THE UNTOLD STORY OF THE LAST AMERICAN MILITARY PRESENCE OF THE VIETNAM WAR

WAR IN OUR WAKE

JONATHAN MALAY

iUniverse®

WAR IN OUR WAKE
The Untold Story of the Last American Military Presence of the Vietnam War

All photographs were taken by the author or by his shipmates, or are in the public domain, or are used with permission.

Cover artwork design is by Stewart Hopewell.

This is a work of nonfiction, but it is not intended to be a scholarly history book. Rather, it is the author's sincere effort to accurately present, for the most part as a first person narrative, the real-life characters and events of a true story. Some liberties are taken in revealing dialog, but if the contents of this book otherwise vary from documented and verifiable fact, it is purely unintentional.

iUniverse books may be ordered through booksellers or by contacting:

iUniverse
1663 Liberty Drive
Bloomington, IN 47403
www.iuniverse.com
1-800-Authors (1-800-288-4677)

ISBN: 978-1-5320-1629-5 (sc)
ISBN: 978-1-5320-1630-1 (e)

Library of Congress Control Number: 2017901422

Print information available on the last page.

iUniverse rev. date: 02/09/2017

To Sharon – My Lady on the Pier.

Metaphors

bitter end: n. 1. the conclusion of a difficult or unpleasant situation. 2. the inboard end of an anchor chain or other line.

Webster's College Dictionary,
Random House 1991

Post umbra lux: After darkness, light.

Motto on the USS Benjamin Stoddert's crest

CONTENTS

Introduction xi

Part One: Setting the Scene

Chapter 1 – A Ship at War 1

Chapter 2 – A Story Waiting to Be Told 7

Chapter 3 – Aloha 13

Chapter 4 – Across the Pacific 31

Chapter 5 – What's In a Namesake? 51

Part Two: Fun and Games

Chapter 6 – The Kid Loves Kimchi 67

Chapter 7 – Land of the Rising Sun 87

Chapter 8 – Christmas Presence 93

Chapter 9 – Subic Special 99

Chapter 10 – An Indian Ocean and African Adventure 111

Chapter 11 – Tedium Denied 127

Chapter 12 – Change of Command 131

Chapter 13 – The Easter Miracle 135

Part Three: This Is the End

Chapter 14 – Pins and Needles 145

Chapter 15 – Welcome to Vietnam 151

Chapter 16 – Time for Reflection.......... 163
Chapter 17 – Beginning the Ending: Operation Frequent Wind ... 175
Chapter 18 – Secret Mission.......... 197
Chapter 19 – Midnight Mayday.......... 207
Chapter 20 – Always the Right Thing to Do 213
Chapter 21 – Steaming Toward Dawn 223
Chapter 22 – The Lady on the Pier 229

Epilog: *Going Down Fighting*.......... 233
A Collection of Images.......... 243
Acknowledgements.......... 251
Sources and Recommended Reading.......... 253

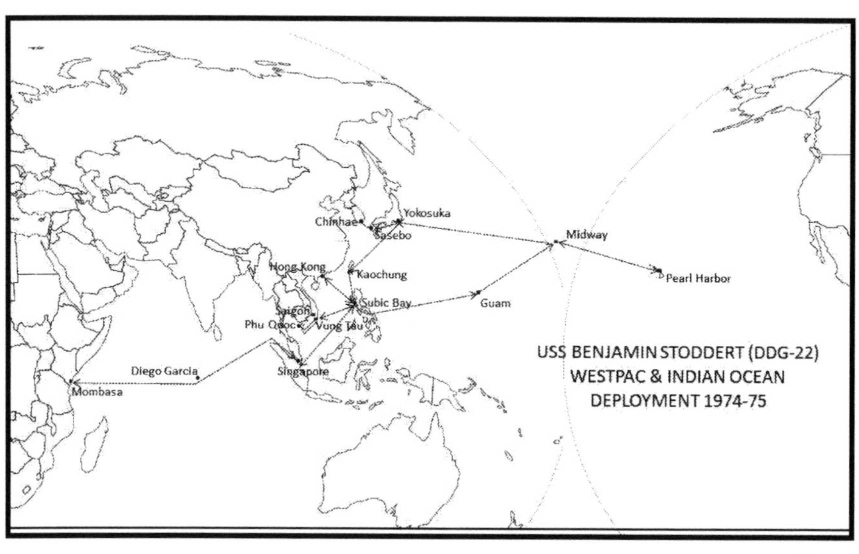

The Voyage: October 1974 – May 1975

INTRODUCTION

This is the end - Beautiful friend
This is the end - My only friend, the end

The Doors: "The End"

Against this haunting music, the opening scene of Francis Ford Coppola's surrealistic 1979 Vietnam War epic "Apocalypse Now" shows what initially is a peaceful coastline of graceful palm trees along a beautiful and deserted beach. As Jim Morrison mournfully sings, helicopters begin to appear and that coast becomes totally engulfed in the violence of bursting explosives and fire. That's the same coast my shipmates and I saw in May, 1975, but with the shelling and fires finally silenced, as we sailed away, leaving a brutal and painful *war in our wake.*

This book relates what it was like to be a witness to the very end of the Vietnam War. It's my personal story, along with a few relevant and hopefully interesting historical notes, of the six and a half month voyage I made as a newly commissioned junior officer aboard the U.S. Navy guided missile destroyer *USS Benjamin Stoddert (DDG-22)*. Although what happened at our deployment's end was truly historic and significant, this is still a sea story from a sailor's perspective. It's my own experiences, and those of my shipmates, that make the history real.

The mid 1970s were a gut-wrenching and painful time for the United States and, of course, for the people of Vietnam. I've done my best to capture the flavor of the end of the "Vietnam era," both at sea and in our visits to various ports in the western Pacific and Indian Oceans. In doing my research, I've culled through our ship's logs and spoken with several of my fellow officers. Perhaps most useful of all, though, were my many letters sent home to my wife, Sharon, in Hawaii, letters she thankfully kept all these years. These letters describe not just what I saw, but also how I felt during this tumultuous period. I've tried very hard to create an accurate narrative of the events our crew experienced, and I've also found it impossible not to make this a love story as well – and that part of the narrative I *know* is true.

After the events of the *Stoddert's* deployment, I went on to complete a full twenty year career of commissioned service in the Navy, most of which I spent in the specialist community of oceanographers and meteorologists. In the last few years of that service, I further specialized in the acquisition, management, and application of space systems for Earth and Space Science, an avocation I carried into a second rewarding and challenging career in the aerospace industry. I began work on this book several years ago but, unfortunately, I had to keep putting the project on the back burner while helping my employer to successfully sell weather satellites and space missions to study the Earth and the sun, and to fly to places like the moon, asteroids, and Jupiter. We also built several scientific missions to Mars, three of which are still at work in orbit around the red planet along with the rovers on the surface for which we built the entry and descent aero-shells. But thankfully, my second retirement has afforded me an opportunity to finish telling this story. My shipmates are anxious to see it finished, particularly since it's a story of finishing things – for better or worse.

I was honored to have had the opportunity to sail with the men you'll meet in this book and to have, with them, a claim on a significant and largely untold slice of history.

I never set out to write a *history* book, destined to be seen only by academics and naval history enthusiasts. Instead, I wanted to create a narrative history that would be read by a broad audience who would enjoy both a good sea story and the very last few pages that haven't previously been written in the long volume of history of America's involvement in the Vietnam War. It was necessary, and I believe useful, to also provide a historical context for the development and warfighting capability of ships like ours, and also for The Honorable Benjamin Stoddert of Maryland, our ship's little remembered but incredibly distinguished namesake.

Being both a sailor and a scientist created a challenge for me to decide on certain conventions to use in this book. You'll see I don't use ALL CAPS in spelling ships' names, even though that practice is usually the standard for military use. I do this simply because I like the way ship names in upper and lower case letters in italics look in print. But the sailor in me has chosen to use the convention of citing nautical miles instead of kilometers for distances sailed, the international standard of metric measurements now found in most books these days. For non-seagoing readers, a nautical mile is exactly 2,000 yards, a nice round number which is admittedly rare in the American system of measurements.

The yard, of course, is equal to three feet or thirty-six inches, and under the terms of the 1959 agreement between the United States, the United Kingdom, and other Commonwealth nations, the "international yard" was legally defined as exactly 0.9144 meter. A yard may also very well have been the legendary distance between Henry I of England's thumb and his nose at the beginning of the 12th Century. But what's more important is that a nautical mile or 2,000 yards is exactly one 60th of a degree of latitude, also known as one minute of latitude. A minute of latitude is the exact same length everywhere on the planet, whereas degrees of longitude are longer at the equator, diminishing to zero length at the Earth's poles. Use of latitude minutes/yards is eminently useful for marine navigation, in the form of 1 minute of latitude = 1 nautical mile = 2,000 yards, which is about 1.85 kilometers.

Don't get me wrong: as a trained scientist, I'm a huge fan of the metric system and was personally disappointed when the United States dropped a federal government initiative to adopt the internationally accepted metric system after Congress, also in 1975, passed the "Meter Conversion Act." I consider the failure to do so pretty much the result of a lack of guts on the part of the government when the effort was abandoned in the 1980s. But as a sailor and as an American, I'm sticking with yards and nautical miles for this story when referring to over-water distances. And, for consistency, when describing distances over land, I'll use the more traditional measurement of statute miles, each of which is 1,760 yards or about 0.87 nautical mile and about 1.6 kilometers. I apologize for going into all this detail, but those who would wish me to use the metric system will hopefully show this sailor some forbearance.

At the risk of further belaboring this point, let's not forget that when measuring depth at sea, a "fathom" is six feet. One may also find it interesting that for distance, the arcane word "league" comes from an ancient Roman measurement of about how far a person could walk in an hour. Although this will be the only mention of the word league in this book, at least in this context, it generally means three nautical miles. So in Jules Verne's classic story of the fabulous but fictitious submarine *Nautilus,* "20,000 Leagues Under the Sea," he was describing a very long, wondrous, and danger-filled voyage of 60,000 nautical miles. That's a fantastical distance, sufficient to circumnavigate the world a few times over. And it's a far longer voyage than that sailed by the *USS Benjamin Stoddert* on the cruise recounted in this book, which took us on our own adventure from Hawaii to Japan, South Korea, Taiwan, the Philippines, and even all the way to Kenya before bringing us to a fateful visit to the coast of Vietnam.

Welcome aboard.

PART ONE:
Setting the Scene

CHAPTER 1

A Ship at War

SAIGON (AP) - South Vietnamese forces lost two more bases in their northernmost province today as U.S. air and naval forces hit the invading North Vietnamese. The South Vietnamese commander in the north said the enemy invasion across the demilitarized zone had been stopped after five days. But Associated Press correspondent Holger Jensen reported from the front that the South Vietnamese navy abandoned its northern base at the mouth of the Cua Viet River Monday night after three days of heavy enemy attacks.

Winona Daily News, Winona, Minnesota, April 4, 1972

In the spring of 1972, when I was still a year away from graduating from the Naval Academy and two years before I reported aboard the *USS Benjamin Stoddert*, the public had long soured on our involvement in Vietnam, but our nation's commitment to the war continued. The war had become like fly paper we couldn't escape. U.S. Navy ships of the Seventh Fleet were operating off the coast of Vietnam, as they had been for years, and one of those was the *USS Benjamin Stoddert (DDG-22),* on her fifth deployment to WestPac.

On the morning of April 17, after taking on tons of five inch shells and supplies from the ammunition ships *USS Pyro* and *USS Haleakala* in a two-step underway replenishment, *Stoddert* set out with the cruiser *Oklahoma City* to conduct a raid on the North Vietnamese port of Vinh. Because the U.S. had, by that time, mined or blockaded the major ports of the North, supply ships from China, often as small as sampans or disguised as fishing boats, used to deliver food and ammunition to their Communist allies by slipping into coastal inlets such as Vinh, which were too numerous to mine or completely blockade. The town was a few miles upstream on a small but navigable river about a hundred and sixty miles south of Hanoi. As she closed in on the shoreline at the river's mouth, the *Stoddert's* electronic sniffing equipment alerted the Combat Information Center that a fire control radar onshore had locked onto *Stoddert.* Almost immediately, two missiles lifted off from shore, probably set to home in on *Stoddert's* own guns' fire control radar, which was active and radiating as she was at battle stations with guns ready to fire. Fortunately, both missiles missed the ship, one exploding fifty yards from her starboard side and the other detonating well astern. Folklore has it that the petty officer at the controls of the ship's fire control radar, seeing with horror the incoming missiles, physically ducked, a motion that depressed the ship's radar beam into the sea and caused the missiles to lose their lock and miss. The ship had literally dodged a bullet… twice. What followed was a thirteen minute gun duel, with *Stoddert* firing salvos from her fore and aft guns and dodging incoming shells, including some whose fragments sprayed the ship but did no damage.

The near miss of those missiles and the vicious but inconclusive gun battle off that river mouth was a reminder and a warning that coastal bombardment was a very dangerous occupation. Over the next several days, *Stoddert* continued to conduct gun fire missions against coastal targets up and down the North Vietnamese coast, as far north as Tranh Hoa, eighty miles south of the capital. This operation was part of "Operation Freedom Train," a coordinated American and South Vietnamese attack which included gunfire bombardments from the sea on the North's logistics infrastructure. Firing all day and re-supplying from ammunition ships by night, *Stoddert* was pounding the coastal region with hundreds of shells and, so far, successfully evading the ineffective communist gunfire directed back at her.

On April 23, though, the North Vietnamese gunners ashore got lucky. *Benjamin Stoddert* took a direct hit on her port bow, causing a fire in the adjacent windlass room, but fortunately there were no crew casualties. The enemy shell landed right on one of the 2's of her white 22 ship's numbering on the bow, briefly altering her appearance to that of the first ship of her class, the *USS Charles F. Adams (DDG-2).* The damage was quickly fixed in a two week repair and refitting port visit at Subic Bay, Philippines, where the United States operated sprawling naval ship and aircraft bases and a shipyard complex. By early June, she was out of the shipyard and back on the gun line seeking to interdict Chinese supply ships along the inlets of the North Vietnamese coast.

Then tragedy came aboard, but not at the hands of the enemy. In the third week of June, the ship was again firing her guns over the North Vietnamese shoreline in support of American and South Vietnamese inland ground forces. They were participating in an operation designed to halt the North Vietnamese army's thrust into the south. At 9:10 on the morning of June 26, she had already been on station for a couple of hours when the ship's forward 5-inch gun was commanded to fire. However, the propulsive charge failed to go off, leaving a live shell in the barrel. They had experienced a misfire.

Inside the gun was an unexploded package of four different explosive charges: the firing primer, a small charge which was supposed to ignite the much larger propulsive charge; the propulsive charge itself, which was a cylindrical silk fabric sack filled with what was essentially black powder which would explode and push the shell at very high velocity out of the barrel and on a ballistic flight to its target; the high explosive in the shell's warhead; and its primer, which would be triggered by either contact with or proximity to a target, according to the design of that particular shell type. And so, inside *Stoddert's* barrel, which was extremely hot from hours of continuous shooting, were four dangerous explosive devices. A misfire was always a bad thing, but it was much worse when the gun barrel was hot enough to fry breakfast on.

The gun crew, the men who were physically inside the structure of the mount, knew there was a chance the shell could "cook off," which means one of the four explosive devices would overheat and simply explode. Now, if it was the propulsive charge that blew up first and the gun's breach (the opening near the base of the barrel into which a shell and powder charge were placed prior to firing) was closed, the gun would simply "go off," sending the shell out the barrel and landing safely away from the ship. But, if the shell itself was to explode in the barrel, the entire explosive bundle would go *kaboom*, and take the whole gun mount along with it. This was a worst case scenario and a constant threat in a hot gun misfire. The countermeasures designed to prevent a gun explosion were to either: (a) open the breach, quickly pull out the shell and powder casing, and throw everything over the side; or (b) cool the barrel as quickly as possible using fire hoses and then try to figure out how to remove the explosives, or try again to fire the gun when everything was cool. The sailors instinctively, but no doubt with the approval of the captain and the officer of the deck looking down from the bridge just aft and above the gun, broke out fire hoses and began to cool the gun's exterior, but they made the mistake of also spraying water into the open end of the barrel in an effort to cool it from both inside and outside. Meanwhile, the ship's weapons department head, Lieutenant Commander Michael Martin, who was at the time manning the gun director (its fire control radar) located above and behind the bridge, was shouting stern orders over the radio for the gun crew to get the breach open, pull out the shell and powder, throw them over the side, and get back to work firing the gun. Understandably, the crew was extremely reluctant to open the breach and expose themselves to a potentially uncontained explosion in their faces.

Lieutenant Commander Martin was reportedly so unhappy at the crew's hesitation that he said he was on his way down there and made it clear it would be very bad news for the men if his orders weren't being carried out by the time he got there. And he did get there, just in time to be entering the gun mount's open door when the crew opened the breach. There was a huge explosion. Lieutenant Commander Martin was expelled by a tremendous force backward out of the mount and through the steel lifelines, killing him instantly. Inside the gun mount, Senior Chief Gunners Mate Gordon Uhler and Gunners Mate first class Robert Mills died instantly. Seaman David Larson was outside the gun manning a hose, and, though he survived being thrown against the superstructure, he died a short time later of massive internal injuries.

In the aftermath, it was determined that the water poured down the barrel had prevented any of the explosive expansion of gases to exit the gun by that route. When the breech was opened inside the gun mount, everyone nearby fell victim to the explosion. Four gallant lives were lost in the incident.

The war went on, as did the ship's mission. A month later, after replacing the gun and repairing all of the other related damage at Subic Bay, *Benjamin Stoddert* was back conducting hot fire missions off of the North Vietnamese coast. By then, the Republic of Vietnam army had taken Quang Tri Province and the North Vietnamese forces had been driven back toward the demilitarized zone (DMZ). There were no more accidents or enemy hits on the ship. As she completed her deployment and headed home to Hawaii at the end of September, 1972, the naval campaign against the north was finally winding down. Exactly four months later, the Paris Accords were signed on January 27, 1973, ending America's warfighting operations. Except for diplomatic and military advisory and security personnel, American forces were withdrawn from Vietnam, and *Benjamin Stoddert* and other warships of the Pacific fleet were given a rest. Although she returned to the theater six months later, there were no more combat operations. What took their place was a mission of "peacetime" patrols, flag-showing, and training exercises during a time of defense spending cutbacks and a Mideast oil embargo in the aftermath of the 1973 Israeli-Arab War, all resulting in decreased time spent underway.

The ship, a proud and battle-scarred member of Pearl Harbor's "Pineapple Fleet," was entering a new phase of her service, but nobody could have known this service would return the ship to Vietnam.

CHAPTER 2

A Story Waiting to Be Told

SAIGON, South Vietnam (AP) - Buddhists gathered Saturday at pagodas here and the northern city of Hue to launch a movement to end the fighting in South Vietnam. Antigovernment demonstrations reportedly planned for today in the Saigon area by Roman Catholics failed to materialize, however, but in Hue new banners went up denouncing President Nguyen Van Thieu's administration. In the face of mounting political dissent against Thieu, North Vietnamese forces struck hard southeast of Hue, triggering fighting that lasted all day Saturday, the Saigon command said. And Radio Hanoi broadcast propaganda calling for the South Vietnamese to overthrow Thieu.

Oakland Tribune, Oakland, California, Sunday, September 15, 1974

Missing from Vietnam War history books is any significant mention of the *United States Ship (USS) Benjamin Stoddert (DDG-22)*, a *Charles F. Adams (DDG-2)*-class guided missile destroyer whose home port was Pearl Harbor, Hawaii. The *Adams,* first of a new class of destroyers, was named after Charles F. Adams, III, who had served as Secretary of the Navy from 1929-1933. *Benjamin Stoddert* was also named after a Secretary of the Navy, the *first* Secretary of the Navy, in fact, and his story will be told a little later in this book. But the ship's story, arguably the last page in that war's history, has been waiting over four decades to be told. Somebody had to be the last Americans to leave Vietnam at the bitter end of the war, and, with no disrespect intended, arguably it wasn't the Marines who boarded the last helicopter to lift off from the rooftop of the American Embassy in Saigon on April 30, 1975. Rather, it was we, the *Stoddert's* crew. On Saturday, May 3, we sailed away from the coast of a unified Vietnam, an ended war behind us. We didn't know it, but we were quietly making history.

The ship's very apt and endearing nickname was the *Benny Sweat*, and it was my incredibly good fortune that *"the Sweat"* was my first sea assignment as the ship's first lieutenant. This meant I was the division officer for the Boatswain (Bos'n) Mates of the deck division, which was officially known as first division and was part of the ship's weapons department, alongside the gun, missile, and antisubmarine warfare divisions. Every naval officer should probably have first lieutenant as their first job because there's no better crucible for learning both seamanship and leadership.

After four years at the U.S. Naval Academy in Annapolis, Maryland and a year of graduate studies in Meteorology at the Naval Postgraduate School in Monterey, California, the *Benny Sweat* took me on the great adventure of my very first deployment to the western Pacific (known to all sailors simply as WestPac). This story is a narrative of our entire deployment, from the day we left home port on November 12, 1974, until the day we returned to that same pier in Pearl Harbor on May 21, 1975, and our many exploits in between. It isn't only about our being the last ship to leave Vietnam. It's also a narrative of what it was like to be part of a young all-male crew on a Vietnam-era deployment to WestPac. Today's Navy is very different, with mixed gender crews, strict rules for conduct ashore, and turn-the-key-and-go gas turbines burning nice clean jet fuel instead of steam boilers that took hours to light off and burned a thick black goop called Navy Special Fuel Oil.

Today, even though naval service at sea is still very demanding, sailors have internet connectivity, high definition TV, and many other modern conveniences. My story captures the sweat-filled adventure and angst of Navy life forty years ago, both at sea and on liberty ashore in exotic Asian and African ports.

Stoddert was a proud ship which wore, on her bridge wings, a prolific assortment of campaign decorations from Vietnam War service, having seen a good share of action in coastal waters "on the gun-line." Over the course of several deployments to Vietnam, she had showered thousands of five inch diameter shells – and death – onto and over the coastline, often sailing right up into the Mekong Delta. And death had come to visit her as well in the tragic explosion of her forward gun mount back in 1972, killing several crewmembers. By the fall of 1974, when *Stoddert* left Pearl Harbor on what was supposed to be a "normal" peacetime deployment to WestPac, the United States had withdrawn in early 1973 from active combat in the war. But the Communist government in the north quickly began to ignore the terms of the armistice brokered by Henry Kissinger and North Vietnamese diplomat Le Duc Tho, betting correctly that the Americans had had enough. So the violent fighting between the People's Republic of Vietnam (PRV) and the Republic of Vietnam (RVN) to its south had gone on. And it was about to come to a tragic end in the following spring, as Communist forces from the north battered the South Vietnamese Army (ARVN), closed in, and engulfed Saigon.

Operation Frequent Wind was the official code name assigned to the evacuation of Saigon. It involved a massive airlift of Americans trapped there, along with thousands of Republic of Vietnam loyalists desperately needing rescue from the approaching North Vietnamese who would surely have killed or imprisoned them. There were also some Vietnamese who were evacuated because they had simply bought their way out and others who just happened to be incredibly lucky to escape. While the media of the day, and historians since then, captured many vivid images and dramatic stories from this final operation of the war, the *USS Benjamin Stoddert* crew's unique and heroic experience was barely recorded.

Operation "Eagle Pull," a smaller in scope and highly classified operation, involved the evacuation of Americans and "friendlies" from Cambodia. Any American presence in Vietnam's neighbor had always been extremely sensitive since Cambodia was technically neutral in the war. *Stoddert* played a role in Eagle Pull, and that aspect of our mission was partially the reason for our being the last to leave Vietnam. But that's only part of this story.

This book doesn't attempt to explain how or why America got entangled in that ugly mess. I assume the reader knows something about the war, which actually began two decades earlier in French-governed Indochina as a conflict between the Chinese- and Soviet Union-backed Communist North Vietnam (Democratic Republic of Vietnam) and the American-backed South Vietnam (Republic of Vietnam). The U.S. had conducted increasingly violent combat operations from 1964 until 1973 on the side of the Republic of Vietnam, resulting in over 58,000 American deaths in the fighting. The People's Army of Vietnam (PRV), of course, ultimately overran Saigon and unified the country under a Communist flag in 1975. I will, however, attempt to illustrate what was happening in Vietnam during the *Stoddert's* deployment through news clippings pulled from American home town newspapers, which will introduce each chapter. As 1974 ended and 1975 began, the military and political conditions in South Vietnam were deteriorating quickly. By that spring, it was clear to the U.S. government that the end was near and Saigon was about to fall without American intervention, which Congress was unwilling to approve. And so we, along with every available ship in the WestPac theater, were dispatched to the coast of Vietnam to await the inevitable, although we had no idea what our role would actually be.

The mission the *USS Benjamin Stoddert* undertook at the war's end secured for our warship, our hardworking young crew, and our unsung commanding officer a little-known place in history. There was the recovery of the floating body of a U.S. airman when there should have been no more American casualties; a sonar search for evidence that would help explain the widely publicized tragedy of an Air Force jumbo transport's crash, which killed one hundred and eighty war orphans, crewmembers, and nurses; a secret mission along the Vietnam coast to rendezvous with a mysterious rubber boat coming out of Cambodia; a surreal encounter with a merchant vessel over-laden with refugees; a midnight encounter with a slowly sinking Republic of Vietnam Navy gunboat; the heartbreak of leaving behind our beautiful young wives and, for many of the crew, their precious children as well; a constantly nagging concern about dwindling fuel; and, in the end, the courageous life or death decision by our commanding officer, who risked his command and the brilliant career that lay ahead of him, to save many, many lives.

Not every sea story is an epic and many are forgotten except in fuzzy reminiscences among sailors over a few beers. But through several reunions of our now gray-haired crew and today's social media connectivity, some of my shipmates and I have come to realize the significance of our experiences. At the same time, though, the passage of many years and America's focus on the difficult and elusive ends of the *new* wars we've been fighting have obscured the country's memory of the end of the war in Vietnam. Thankfully, though, our memory was recently refreshed with Rory Kennedy's searing 2014 documentary "Last Days in Vietnam." Unfortunately, Ms. Kennedy's excellent and critically acclaimed film was not informed by the *whole* story. So this is my attempt at providing a firsthand recollection of *our* story, as well as to provide additional details about the *Benjamin Stoddert's* Vietnam War mission prior to my assignment to the ship, as told in the previous chapter.

CHAPTER 3

Aloha

WASHINGTON (AP) – President Ford will hold a news conference to be broadcast on television and radio from the East Room at 8:00 p.m. EDT today, a spokesman said. The session will be the second of Ford's five-week-old presidency and comes the same day as he signed executive orders implementing his program of clemency for Vietnam-era draft evaders and deserters. Questioning of the President is certain to focus on his controversial pardon for former President Richard M. Nixon.

The Daily Leader, Pontiac Illinois, September 16, 1974

That I chose to serve in the Navy and to later become a specialist in ocean and atmospheric science was sort of inevitable. Although I was born in the White Mountains town of Littleton, New Hampshire, my family moved to Beverly Farms, Massachusetts on the North Shore coast when I was only five. My dad was a tobacco and "sundries" salesman and he asked his company to change his territory to the Bay State so his three sons, of which I was the youngest, could attend St. John's Preparatory School, aka "the Prep," a respected Catholic high school in nearby Danvers. Also, my mom's sister and her family lived in Prides Crossing, right next door to Beverly Farms, with both "townships" being part of the city of Beverly, and the sisters had always been close. We three guys did, in fact, all get to go to the Prep and I did well there, earning good grades, playing football and track, and learning discipline from the usually tough Brothers of St. Francis Xavier. I discovered that I loved math and science, and also that I was totally smitten by a girl named Sharon who was the sister of my best friend, Peter Healey. The Healey's, a big Irish family with five kids, lived in Marblehead and Sharon went to Bishop Fenwick, another Catholic high which was nearby in Peabody. More will be said about Beverly, Marblehead, and Sharon later in this book.

Growing up on the North Shore gave me a chance to spend a lot of time with, and to love, the ocean. At our town's beach, if we could stand the usually too cold water, we could dive or cannonball from a high diving board on the pier, or snorkel around the rocks to catch our own lobsters, or cast our lines for the then-abundant flounder, pollock, and mackerel. The ocean was an important part of my life. And whenever the Prep had a career night, I always enjoyed listening to the oceanography grad students that had been invited to come up from Woods Hole Oceanographic Institution on Cape Cod. While I wasn't particularly excited by their stories of counting plankton – which sounded boring – I enjoyed hearing them talk about their research ship expeditions to collect specimens and make observations of such things as salinity and ocean temperature, as well as weather observations. The fact that all the visiting oceanography students were attractive young ladies was also appealing. I was hooked.

Although he seemed to never want to talk about it very much, my dad was very proud that he had served in the Navy during World War II, eventually reaching the rank of fireman first class. He had survived the war as a diesel technician on small destroyer escorts, first in the Atlantic and then in the South Pacific. No doubt, he had plenty of war stories to tell, but he seemed to have put all that behind him. But he did make it clear to his sons that he'd be proud if any of us chose to serve in the military, and particularly in the Navy.

On at least one occasion, I remember dad telling my brothers Bob, Joe, and me that if we ever consider serving, we should think carefully about which service to join. I remember him saying something like, "Guys, I want you to visualize yourself sitting in a hole in the ground, in a cold rain, eating cold food out of a can. Now, visualize yourself in a dry uniform, standing on a steel deck aboard ship, with three hot meals a day and a warm dry bed to sleep in. Then decide which service you want to join."

And so by my junior year, I decided that I'd like to go to sea in ships and study the ocean, even though I had no idea how I'd ever make that happen. But then my dad mentioned to me that he had a friend whose son had attended the United States Merchant Marine Academy at King's Point, New York, and maybe I should check it out. That was it… no pushing, no reminder we were a blue collar family with very meager financial resources, and no stating the obvious that I wasn't going to get a football scholarship to college like my very big older brothers, who both went to Tufts University on scholarships. But he knew it was probably enough. So, knowing all those things which meant I wasn't going to Harvard, I sent away for a catalog from King's Point. I read it over and over until the pages were warn, and I learned a few things which were very attractive. It's free. They did teach oceanography. Graduates serve in the Merchant Marine. You get a U.S. Navy Reserve commission. And, not insignificantly since the Vietnam War was going on, it was very likely I'd never be drafted and never get shot at. And so, I applied to my Congressman for a nomination to King's Point, but on all of the paperwork for my application, including forms I filled out at my physical exam at the Chelsea Naval Hospital in Boston, I discovered I could check off other national service academies to which I might want my application to also apply. In addition to the U.S. Merchant Marine Academy, I checked off the U.S. Naval Academy.

One evening in October of my senior year, a couple of months after submitting my application package to the Congressman, I received a call from his office. The staff member with whom I was speaking congratulated me on having been selected for a nomination to King's Point, but he also asked if I would be interested in accepting the Congressman's Principal Nomination to the Naval Academy. I asked, "Does that mean if I say yes, I'll go?" It seemed as if he chuckled a bit and then said, "Mr. Malay, Congressman Bates serves on the House Armed Services Committee, and all his nominees to all the military academies actually get into them." Right then and there, without hesitation, I accepted the nomination to Annapolis. I've never regretted it. Never once since then have I visited King's Point or given it a second thought. And four and half years later, on June 6, 1973, I was an Annapolis graduate with a degree in oceanography and a commission as an Ensign, United States Navy.

Right after graduation, I married Sharon, my high school sweetheart, and headed off to Monterey, California, for a one-year Master of Science degree in Meteorology at the Naval Postgraduate School. It turned out that while studying oceanography at the academy, I confirmed my high school suspicion I wouldn't much like counting plankton, and didn't enjoy chemistry very much either. So I had taken every elective offered in the field of meteorology and chose to study it for my master's degree since it was essentially all math and physics, both of which I loved and did well in. The year I spent in grad school gave Sharon and me a chance to enjoy being newlyweds, and for me to grow a beard and not think too much about what would happen right after graduation, namely assignment to sea duty.

I've never liked the term "snotty-nosed Ensign" as a description of a newly commissioned naval officer. It says, "This kid doesn't even know enough to wipe his own nose." But as a U.S. Navy Ensign on Monday, September 16, 1974, I would have said I actually did know quite a lot about the Navy and about the sea from my four years as an oceanography major at the Naval Academy. As a Midshipman on summer training cruises, I had crossed the Atlantic and back on an amphibious assault aircraft carrier and sailed the Caribbean on an attack submarine. And I guess I couldn't have been too dumb, having just completed a one year Master of Science program in meteorology at the Naval Postgraduate School in Monterey, California and then three months of antisubmarine warfare and nuclear weapons handling schools in San Diego. But deep down inside, I was also astute enough to know I still had a tremendous amount to learn about how to be a naval officer, and how to be a leader. That opportunity to learn what *really* mattered in the Navy had finally arrived, and, having spent so much time in classrooms, I was ready to report to my first ship and start my on-the-job training in the real world.

A first assignment to sea duty is an exciting thing. And, with no small amount of apprehension that mid-September day, this snotty-nosed Ensign reported aboard the *USS Benjamin Stoddert (DDG-22)* at her home port of Pearl Harbor, Hawaii. Sharon and I had arrived at Honolulu International Airport on Oahu on the previous day with nothing but our suitcases and the anticipation that the adventure of a lifetime was just about to begin. Sharon's challenge was in making a home for us in a Navy-assigned cinder block one bedroom housing unit in a community of nearly identical units just mauka (mountain-side vs. ocean-side) of Kamehameha Highway across from the airport. She accomplished this beautifully with nothing more than worn-out Navy-loaned furniture, a talent for style-on-a-budget accessorizing, and a great attitude. For me, it was exciting to walk up the brow (gangplank) of a beautiful – in the eyes of this beholder – armed-to-the-teeth warship, tied up at Bravo Pier at the Pearl Harbor Naval Station. Dressed in my starched Summer White uniform, with my hair and grad school-grown beard neatly trimmed, I smartly saluted the American flag flying at the stern, and then saluted the officer of the deck, saying the traditional words: "Request permission to come aboard, sir." Upon receiving the cursory reply, "Granted," and identifying myself, I was quickly escorted to the stateroom of executive officer (XO) Lieutenant Commander Parker T. Finch. The XO was a slightly-built, erudite-looking gentleman with short cropped hair and Navy-issue black rimmed glasses. My first impression of him was that of a young college professor. But he was very welcoming and said they'd been looking forward to my arrival because there was a lot of work to be done and I had a group of men waiting for their new division head. Then he took me to meet our commanding officer, Commander Edward A. Siegrist. He was "the CO" or "the captain," since commanding officers at sea are always called captain regardless of their actual rank. (The informal title "Skipper" is also sometime used, but that's incorrect since Skipper is the term for the officer in charge of a small boat such as a World War II PT Boat whose commanding officer is in charge of a squadron of several such boats.) As I shook Captain Siegrist's hand, there we were, the two officers in the ship's wardroom on either ends of the saltiness spectrum; one who knew more about the sea, ships, war, and sailors than anyone else on board, and one who knew almost nothing about the real world of the Navy. But I was about to learn from a master.

My initial reaction to meeting the CO was actually pretty close to awe. Commander Ed Siegrist was a new kind of leader I'd only seen once before on a short midshipman summer cruise two years earlier on the fast attack submarine *USS Pargo (SSN-650)*. The difference was that Dave Hinkle on *Pargo* and Ed Siegrist on *Stoddert* were *commanding officers.* Captain Siegrist bore the sole and inescapable responsibility for the physical property of his ship and its contents and, more importantly, for the lives of crew assigned to her. This man was also charged with the power to unleash the arsenal of weaponry the ship possessed, up to and including the capability to launch rocket-thrown nuclear depth charges. He towered over his executive officer and even stood two or three inches above my five feet, ten inches. He was what you'd call "a big man." He had a big frame, a big right hand that nearly crushed mine, and a big, warm smile. I also came to learn the man had a huge heart, which manifested itself in a personality of authority without intimidation and competence without arrogance. He was a man I watched and listened to closely, imitated whenever I could, and deeply respected.

About the ship: *Benjamin Stoddert* was a destroyer (which are normally numbered with the designation "DD"), but she was equipped with a surface-to-air missile (SAM) system, making her a *guided missile* destroyer, hence her designation as a "DDG." In the 1970's she was second in firepower only to much larger missile-equipped destroyer leaders (DLGs), cruisers (CGs), and, of course, battleships (BBs). Although they had been brought back from mothballs into service for Vietnam and again later in the 1980's, there were no BBs in service at that time. *Stoddert* was armed with a single-rail TARTAR SAM launcher aft, fore and aft five-inch guns, an eight-missile capacity Antisubmarine Rocket (ASROC) launcher (which had the capability of launching both rocket-thrown nuclear depth charges or rocket-thrown Mark 46 torpedoes), and port and starboard triple-cell Mark 32 torpedo tubes. Measuring 437 feet in length and displacing (the nautical way of saying "weighing") 3,277 tons before being fully loaded with a nominal crew of about 350, fuel for both her steam boilers and diesel auxiliaries, a motor whaleboat, a captain's gig, ammunition, and stores, she was a powerful ship brisling with weapons.

In World War II, destroyers were lightly armored antisubmarine warfare ships equipped with either three- or five-inch guns (or both) and racks of barrel-shaped depth charges. They were very fast, capable of speeds in excess of thirty knots. But as relatively small ships, often referred to as "tin cans," or "greyhounds of the sea," or "small boys," they were also somewhat expendable, relative to the battleships and aircraft carriers. One of the most inspirational stories of destroyers in action came in the penultimate World War II Pacific theater battle of Leyte Gulf, arguably called the largest, and certainly the last, fleet battle in history. From that battle, there is a great story of one destroyer, the *USS Johnston,* a *Fletcher*-class ship led by Commander Ernest E. Evans, a Native American from Oklahoma who rose to command against tremendous odds. Evans earned his place in history by steering his hopelessly outsized warship into the Japanese fleet at flank speed. Vice Admiral Clifton A. F. Sprague, the American commander of Task Unit 77.4.3, also known by its code name Taffy 3, took notice and ordered his destroyer assets: "Small boys attack!" *Johnston*, and the destroyers *Hoel* and *Heerman,* together with the even smaller destroyer escort *Samuel B. Roberts,* aggressively attacked the Japanese formation of cruisers and battleships, including the massive and powerful battleship *Yamato,* with fearless suicidal determination. The Japanese commander, Admiral Takeo Kurita, reportedly believing he was being attacked by a force of major "heavy" warships, broke off the action. The fleet battle pitting Kurita against Admiral Bull Halsey, Commander of the Third Fleet, still had several acts to be played out, but the momentum had shifted to the Americans. The *USS Johnston* ultimately succumbed to heavy damage and sank. Captain Evans died shortly afterwards from his wounds and was posthumously awarded the Medal of Honor for his heroism. The American destroyers had earned an important place in the history of naval warfare.

During the 1950s and 1960s, destroyers didn't change much. They were still armed with sonar and antisubmarine weapons and with gun mounts fore and aft, and some were converted to radar picket ships and re-designated as DDR's. Others were designated as ASW destroyer escorts, or DDE's. Later, many were overhauled in shipyards in the Fleet Rehabilitation and Modernization (FRAM) program, which increased their size and outfitted them with better sensors and upgraded weapons. "FRAM Cans" were becoming the backbone of the destroyer fleet and continued to be fast and potent weapon systems as the U.S. Navy expanded its presence in Southeast Asia.

In July, 1964, the *USS Maddox (DD-731)*, a 21 year old pre-FRAM *Allen M. Sumner*-class destroyer, was conducting signals intelligence collection in the international waters of the Tonkin Gulf off the coast of Vietnam when it was aggressively approached by three North Vietnamese Navy (NVN) motor torpedo boats. Captain John Herrick, the Seventh Fleet Destroyer Division commander aboard the *Maddox*, ordered Commander Herbert Ogier, the ship's commanding officer, to fire on the gunboats if they came within five nautical miles of the ship. When they did breach this distance, *Maddox* fired three rounds of warning shots to send a signal to the NVN boats that they should break off their approach. Instead of withdrawing, the torpedo boats attacked, firing their torpedoes at maximum range, but fortunately they did not hit the *Maddox.* But their attack touched off a vigorous defensive action by the Americans. The combined effect of gunfire from the destroyer and the arrival of attacking F-8 Crusaders from the nearby American aircraft carrier *USS Ticonderoga* resulted in heavy damage to the NVN boats and the wounding and death of a number of NVN sailors, but no U.S. losses. What was lost, however, was America's still passive role in the growing war in Indochina. The Gulf of Tonkin incident, and President Johnson subsequently asking

Congress to authorize the use of force by the U.S. military, were the first steps toward America's future "shooting role" in what we know as the Vietnam War.

One month after the Gulf of Tonkin incident, in September, 1964, the *USS Benjamin Stoddert (DDG-22)* was commissioned at Puget Sound Bridge and Dredging Company in Seattle, Washington. The first of the new class of ships *Stoddert* belonged to, was the *USS Charles F. Adams (DDG-2),* which had been commissioned in 1960. Introduction of the *Adams*-class marked a major step forward in the lethal capabilities of ships of their size. Like the *Fletcher and Sumner*-class, and even the somewhat heavier *Mitscher*-class (later re-designated "Destroyer Leaders" or DLs instead of DDs), *Stoddert* had four 1,200 pounds-per-square-inch pressure Babcock and Wilcox steam boilers driving two General Electric steam turbines and twin propellers. Like them, she had fore and aft five-inch guns (each single-barrel, but very fast-firing), port and starboard three-tube MK 32 torpedo launchers, an eight-cell Antisubmarine Rocket (ASROC) launcher amidships, an AN/SQS-23 sonar, and SPS-10 and SPS-40 radars for surface and air search, respectively. But, unlike earlier destroyers, and similar to the new and much larger guided missile cruisers such as the *USS Leahy*-class, these new destroyers had an aft-mounted TARTAR missile launcher that could help provide anti-aircraft protection for aircraft carriers in addition to their traditional antisubmarine warfare role. This required the ship also to have an SPS-39 three-dimensional air search radar for missile targeting. *Stoddert*, like all *Charles F. Adams*-class DDGs, was heavily armed, and with four boilers, two steam turbine engines, and twin eight foot diameter brass propellers, she was fast and lethal.

That day back in 1974, as I took stock of my first ship, in which my first assignment was to take charge of the Boatswains (Bos'n) Mates, the deck gear and rigging, and the physical appearance of the ship's exterior paint, I could see she was truly beautiful. From her high, sweeping, curved "hurricane bow," to her raked twin smoke stacks, to the low helicopter deck on her fantail (for hovering and lowering of passengers and supplies by cable only – the deck being too small for actually landing aircraft), she was sleek and sexy. As her First Lieutenant, I found myself responsible for keeping her good looking and leading her two dozen ragtag First Division crew of Bos'n Mates and Seamen. As lovable as they were, both the ship and the men would prove to be quite a challenge.

After reporting aboard and meeting the CO and XO and several of the officers, including weapons officer Lieutenant Rick Buttina, my direct boss, I was released to go back ashore and find Sharon. We had much to do to get a Navy family housing unit assigned to us, arrange for the issue of our no frills "loaner" bamboo rattan furniture, go shopping for what we needed first (like beer), and generally ask ourselves what we'd gotten ourselves into. I'd just been told the ship would leave within a few weeks for at least six months on a WestPac deployment. Sharon and I had a million things to do, but that's when I discovered my wife's incredible resourcefulness. My job, she said, was to do my duty aboard ship and trust that she'd be OK. In fact, she was beyond OK. She was fantastic.

We had shipped our bright yellow VW Beetle to Hawaii in advance and picked it up at the Honolulu cargo terminal. On our first couple of weekends, we cruised around the island enjoying the beauty of Oahu's spectacular mountain passes, sugar cane and pineapple fields, and, of course, the beaches. We also enjoyed exploring the night life on Waikiki Beach, where we found a downtown bar we liked. Their mai tais were tasty and the every-night local singer crooned mellow Hawaiian songs and slyly but ruthlessly made fun of the haoles, the (mostly Caucasian) tourists. We also scored a couple of sightings of actor James MacArthur, a bar regular who was at that time playing Detective Danny "Danno" Williams on the original and hugely popular "Hawaii Five-O" TV show. Sharon and I hadn't seen each other very much over that previous year while I was in graduate school and she worked full time as a Registered Dietitian at the local Monterey Peninsula Hospital. But in those short weeks on Oahu before the ship deployed, we were a couple of kids in love, living in paradise, and feeling like a million bucks, even with precious little money in our pockets. It's a good thing the mai tais were cheap and the beaches were free. We lived it up because we knew our time to enjoy each other was short.

By day in this pre-sailing time, I followed my boss Rick Buttina around the ship, pocket notebook and pen in hand, to record and plan for correction his notice of cosmetic blemishes, improperly stowed gear, missing wrenches, out-of-alignment mooring lines, etc. And I spent hours getting to know my fellow crewmates in first division, particularly our crusty, profane Chief Bos'n Mate Tom Spicer. On just my second day aboard, Chief Spicer made it a point, in front of me and several members of the division, to call one of our young African American sailors "boy." The young sailor understandably got very upset. I was sure the Chief was testing me. I immediately asked to speak with him in private and I poked him in the chest with my finger and told him that if he ever did that again, I'd have him before a court martial. After glaring at me for a couple of seconds, he backed off, apologized, and said it wouldn't happen again. Then, at my no-compromise direction, he apologized to the young sailor in front of my entire division of enlisted men. I was also blessed by having two First Class Bos'n Mates between the troops and the Chief. One of them was a humungous, good natured native Hawaiian named Silva. (Nobody, including me, ever seemed to use his first name, which is what he clearly preferred.) The other was a wiry six foot five inch tall redneck-but-good-as-gold guy named Charlie Ferris. Both eventually became Chief Petty Officers themselves, but at the time, even though they weren't yet wearing the khaki uniform of a Chief, they were the true enlisted leaders of the division, and I completely trusted them. They were professionals and had earned the right to be addressed by the informal name for a senior Boatswain's Mate: "Boats."

In the age of sail in the American Navy, as in the Royal Navy whose rich heritage we inherited, there were enlisted seamen, and there were commissioned officers. But there was also a cadre of non-commissioned officers or "warrant officers." On sailing ships, the senior non-commissioned navigator and quartermaster was the "Sailing Master," the chief of rigging and discipline was the "Boatswain," and finally there was the critical post of "Carpenter." Rarely would a ship carry a fully trained physician, but every ship had a practitioner of stitching wounds, dosing venereal disease, pulling rotten or shattered teeth, and, of course, the all too common removal of splintered or infected limbs. The individual who, for better or worse, possessed these skills – or at least carried them out as best they could – was "The Surgeon." These positions translated into today's rank of Chief Warrant Officer (CWO), although doctors are now commissioned officers and there's not much need for a carpenter on a steel ship.

Stoddert had two Warrant Officers who lived in "officer country" staterooms and were full members of our wardroom: CWOs Bob Thompson (electronics) and Ed Moon (engineering/ boilers). Like them, the khaki-wearing Chief Petty Officers, who maintained their own "Chiefs Mess," were the other crusty old salts who possessed the experience and expertise to provide technical skills and leadership to the dungaree-wearing "white hats" of the enlisted crew. Our most senior enlisted man was a physically small but tough-as-nails Master Chief Electrician's Mate named Andy Irwin.

CWO's Bob and Ed were colorful characters, but to call any Warrant Officer "colorful" is usually redundant! Bob was more than a little overweight and he always seemed to be suffering from any number of ailments. Among his quirks, he never wore laces in his shoes and was unable to button the top (or bottom) buttons of his khaki shirts. Ed, who had come up through the ranks as a boiler technician and was the senior member of the "snipes" who maintained our four boilers, was a tall, wiry, red-haired man. Neither made any pretense of sophistication, and both had a great sense of humor. I quickly learned to show deference to them and to the Chief Petty Officers while letting them know I was working hard to prove I deserved the respect they were obliged to show me as a commissioned officer.

Lieutenant Rick Buttina was a patient and reasonable boss, always willing to take extra time to help me learn my job, but not letting me slack in anything. A Latin language major from Holy Cross College in Boston, he and I shared Catholic educations and Massachusetts accents, since I had grown up in Beverly Farms, a town on the rocky coast about thirty miles north of Boston. But, unlike my more "casual" approach to neatness, Rick was a classic obsessive compulsive when it came to cleanliness and orderliness – the drawers in his stateroom contained his underwear and socks, perfectly folded and stored in Tupperware containers. And so he insisted both the ship's exterior and interior be as close to perfectly painted and cleaned as possible. I admired him greatly because in spite of his self-discipline and high expectations for his subordinates, he wasn't ever what one could call nasty or overbearing. He showed me that an officer could hold himself and his subordinates to very high standards by personal example and intelligently give direction to his division officers and then trust them to do their jobs without micromanaging. Since I found myself at the receiving end of much of that direction, I learned fast.

But my education began in earnest on Saturday, November 2, 1974, just six short weeks since I'd reported aboard. Sharon and I exchanged last kisses and long embraces, and feigned cheerful Aloha's to hide our sadness and apprehension. She and the other wives and kids were left waving to us from the pier as our mooring lines were taken in and the national ensign was swiftly hauled up to the masthead with the in-port American flag simultaneously pulled down at the stern. With one long blast on the ship's horn signaling "underway," and then three short blasts for "backing down," we slowly slid backwards and away from the pier and then spun around smartly in the channel, pointing toward Ford Island in the middle of Pearl Harbor. Our bow pointed west and, with rudder amidships and both engines ahead one third, we headed for the harbor exit. Instead of turning left immediately and southward toward the sea, I remember we took a wider path so as to pass abreast of the sunken hulk of the *USS Arizona,* sitting on the harbor's bottom alongside the island, with its white memorial structure above it proudly flying the American flag. Since December 7, 1941, *Arizona* has never been decommissioned and is the resting place of most of the 1,177 members of her crew who died during the Japanese attack that brought our country into World War II. As is tradition in the U.S. Navy, we rendered honors to starboard with all hands on deck at attention along the rail and a salute from the bridge. It was a reminder to all of us that *Stoddert* was a warship heading to sea, to do whatever we had to do to protect our nation.

This was a fitting way for us to get our heads in the game as we headed down the shipping channel to the south shore of Oahu and the open sea, but there was one more farewell about to happen. Just as we passed the final tip of land at the exit to the channel, I spotted several women waving to us from the shore. Some of the wives must have jumped into cars and driven down to that vantage point to see us off one more time. And there was Sharon, waving farewell/aloha in her bright red slacks and white top, with her long brown hair resting on her shoulders. We were too far away, though, to each see the tears in both our eyes. She was the last sight I can remember as we headed through the buoys marking the safe passage through the coral reefs, cleared the channel, and turned to steam westward.

My men and I, standing near the bow, forward of the gun mount, looked at each other, said a few words, and then I dismissed them to go below and shift out of their white uniforms and into dungarees. As I headed to my stateroom to change into my khaki uniform, walking along the topside walkway from the forecastle (called the fo'c'sle by old salts), I looked back at our island home and thought about Sharon, now driving home or heading somewhere with her fellow deserted wives, and how much I was going to miss her. But, closing the watertight door behind me as I moved inside the ship, I began to think about all that lay ahead. And since I would soon have to stand my first underway watch on the bridge, apprehension quickly took over: I could handle being lovesick on the job, but not seasick.

My first stop on the way to my stateroom was sick bay where Chief Hospital Corpsman Cordeiro cheerfully gave me an envelope with about a dozen Dramamine pills – the standard preventative for motion sickness – just in case. He said to watch out for drowsiness, its common side effect. I was wide awake and felt physically great, just nervous about what lay ahead. So I thanked the Chief, tucked the pills into my pocket, and hoped I wouldn't need them. I said goodbye and headed below to get changed into my work uniform. There was work to do!

Where we were headed, or so we thought, was just about anywhere in the western Pacific *except* for Vietnam – or China or North Korea, of course. We had just lived through the drama of President Richard M. Nixon's resignation a few months earlier, with an abrupt transition to the short but eventful Presidency of Gerald R. Ford. Secretary of State Henry Kissinger remained in the Ford cabinet, bridging the transition with the political and military situation in Vietnam growing worse. The North Vietnamese had, for a time, more or less abided by the terms of the Paris accords, apparently in fear that Nixon would be willing to bring America back into the war, or at re-start the bombing of the north. But in the summer of 1974, they correctly calculated that President Ford and the American people, reeling from the resignation of a disgraced president and other serious domestic issues, would have no stomach for more fighting by "our American boys" in Vietnam. The Viet Cong were again on the attack. A bad end for the Republic in the south was seemingly inevitable in the view of practically everyone – except for, ironically, U.S. Ambassador to South Vietnam Graham A. Martin, who remained inexplicably optimistic that the situation could be turned around.

Here we were, a powerful warship headed westward across the vast ocean toward a six month mission that had yet to be defined. But we in the crew were highly doubtful our ship, a bloodied veteran of the war, would be brought into action. So I had many things on my mind that day, but Vietnam was not one of them.

CHAPTER 4

Across the Pacific

SAIGON (UPI) - President Nguyen Van Thieu today pleaded for his political life. Thieu promised to fight government corruption, but a leader of the 1963 coup that ousted Ngo Dinh Diem as President said South Vietnam needs new leaders... On the 12th anniversary of the overthrow of Diem, one of the leaders of the coup, Gen. Duong Van "Big" Minh did everything but call for Thieu's resignation. "National reconciliation is a completely new task which requires a new set of leaders, enjoying the backing of the people, sincerely desiring reconciliation and having a capacity for creating the future," Minh said.

Naples Daily News, Naples, Florida, November 1, 1974

As I changed my white uniform into khakis, the ship began to pitch and roll in the seas and swells offshore. I knew in my heart that Sharon would be fine through the deployment, and I'd be OK too. In the short term, though, I was less sure. In my midshipman years, I'd been across the Atlantic to England and Denmark on a large amphibious assault helicopter carrier, and I'd sailed from New London, Connecticut to the Caribbean and back on a nuclear attack submarine, and yet the only time I'd ever been seasick was with Sharon and friends out deep-sea fishing off of Monterey. I remembered Sharon and our friend Cathy Meldrum hauling in more than a dozen good sized fish while Cathy's husband and my Naval Academy classmate Duncan and I puked our guts out. Our wives weren't very impressed with their naval officer husbands! With that memory refreshed in my mind, I wondered how my body would react this time as we began to rise and fall in moderate six foot seas. The ship's movement beneath my feet reminded me I was a true newbie, the least qualified officer for any watch station, and yet I knew I was looking forward to on-the-job training like none other on Earth.

Now that we were underway, my division was humming along in its duties. They were a pretty rough group, but they were hardworking, and I quickly realized I could let Petty Officers Silva and Ferris run the show while Chief Spicer hung out drinking coffee and griping about everything in the Chief's mess. So I got to work learning how to be an officer of the deck.

In 1974, the Chief of Naval Operations was Admiral Elmo R. "Bud" Zumwalt, an officer who had earned an excellent reputation and rapid advances in rank in Vietnam's Mekong Delta. Admiral Zumwalt, or "Zumie" as we often referred to him, was popular in the fleet because he was considered to be a "modern" officer for his day. He had long sideburns and longer than usual hair, neither of which were within the still-on-the-books haircut regulations. He authorized sailors to wear beards, and, with him as an example, haircut regulations were largely ignored. His opinion was it was the work to be done, not the appearance of the sailor doing it, which mattered. In the spirit of these lax grooming standards, my crew of Bos'n Mates were, in general, pretty slack in their personal hygiene. I, myself, had a full beard, as did several of the other junior officers, and I wore my hair longer than the rest of the junior officers. All of the more senior officers such as the department heads, the XO, and the CO were trying to set a good example and were clean shaven, although some had mustaches, and they all had short haircuts.

On the third day at sea, however, it became evident every sailor and many of the officers who didn't already have a beard were starting to grow them, or at least trying to. Later that day, in a huddle with my division, someone threw out the idea that, as a joke, our division – the grubbiest on board – would all shave our beards and get regulation haircuts, including me. We thought it would be hilarious for us to be the most "regulation" and sharp-looking sailors on the ship. And it actually *was* hilarious too… for a couple of days, anyway. When the captain and everybody else saw what we'd done, we were a big hit. And then, of course, we all stopped shaving again after a couple of days.

Junior officers in the engineering department headed by Lieutenant Commander Don Austin stood watches in the engineering compartments below deck. Those in Lieutenant Rick Buttina's weapons department or Lieutenant Eric Utegaard's operations department were assigned to stand watch on either the bridge or in the Combat Information Center (CIC). As a weapons guy, I was scheduled to stand training watches as a junior officer of the deck (JOOD) under instruction on the bridge. The CO generally spent most of his day sitting in his raised high back chair on the starboard side of the bridge working on paperwork brought to him in piles by the Yeomen, the ship's clerks. But, whether or not the captain was present on the bridge, the operation and control of the ship was done by the bridge watch team, all standing on their feet for the entire four hours of the watch (hence the term "watch standers.") The team consisted of: the officer of the deck (OOD); the JOOD (like me); the quartermaster of the watch, who tracked the ship's position on a chart and made entries in the deck log; the boatswain's mate of the watch, who maintained the schedule of events and made announcements when directed over the ship's public address system, known as the 1MC; the contact-plotter, who marked surface contacts' range and bearing with grease pencils on a large Plexiglas "bogey tote board" that would eerily light up at night; a phone talker in contact with other watch-standers all over the ship; the helmsman who steered the course ordered by the OOD or the JOOD, depending on which of them "had the conn"; and finally the lee-helmsman, who stood at the twin-handled speed indicators which, when moved, signaled the engine room to increase or decrease speed, stop, or reverse for each of our two steam engines.

Way down below decks in main control, located in one of the two engine rooms, there was an engineering officer of the watch (EOOW) with a junior EOOW (in training to become an EOOW just as his counterpart on the bridge was learning to be an OOD) and several enlisted engineering watch standers in both engine rooms and both boiler rooms. There was also a Combat Information Center (CIC) watch officer who controlled the ship's sensors and weapons. The CIC on *Stoddert* was located directly behind the bridge. In addition, other watch standers were stationed all over the ship, including sonar men, radar men, radio men, signal men, lookouts, a "sounding and security" engineer who constantly roamed the ship measuring fuel and fresh water levels, a roving (and armed) security guard whose main duty was to ensure the protection of our nuclear depth charge launcher and magazine, and a very lonely guy all the way back in "after steering" near the rudders who was ready to manually move the ship's rudders, as directed by radio commands from the bridge, in the event of a loss of steering control from the helm on the bridge. About one third of the crew was on watch at any given moment, and the rest were either trying to catch some all-too-precious sleep or doing their day jobs of maintenance, cleaning, paperwork, or training.

And so, there I stood on the bridge, for eight hours out of every twenty-four in a three section rotation. The watches ran from 0800-1200 (the forenoon watch); 1200-1600 (the afternoon watch); 1600-1800 (the first dog watch); 1800-2000 (the second dog watch), with these shorter two hour watches designed to allow for two sittings at dinner and a daily rotation so watch teams wouldn't stand the same watches day in and day out; 2000-2400 (the evening watch); 0000-0400 (the mid watch); and, my favorite, 0400-0800 (the morning watch). I actually loved the morning watch because it was usually really quiet, with the captain sure to be asleep, no drills scheduled, and with a glorious dawn to witness. The down side, of course, was that after getting off watch and grabbing a quick breakfast, I had to get to work running my division, studying for my qualifications, and participating in training exercises, and then going back on watch for the first dog watch and then the upcoming mid watch, meaning twenty-four hours pretty much without sleep. On most days, this predictable and grinding routine would be broken by special events such as underway replenishments (known as UNREPs) for refueling or re-supply, fire drills, security alert drills (simulating a threat to our nuclear weapon system), and all-hands general quarters drills in which we simulated missile and torpedo launches, or best of all, when we actually fired our weapons. Nothing says fun to a sailor like tremendous ship-shaking explosions and the pungent smell of cordite when the big guns fire. But not so fun was the deep fatigue that resulted from chronic lack of sleep – we all suffered from it.

Qualifying as JOOD only took about three days of watches because, to be frank, the only job of the JOOD was to learn how to be an OOD from the OOD himself. Most OOD's would assign the JOOD to be the conning officer, referred to as "having the conn," meaning the formal responsibility for verbally ordering the course and speed changes. Such orders by a JOOD with the conn were carefully monitored by the OOD because it was *his* ass on the line if there was an error. I learned to love the job of "driving the ship" up there on the bridge. To me, it was the quintessence of being a naval officer. And I enjoyed standing outside in the open air on the bridge wing, feeling the cold spray of salt water or the clean smell of the wind buffeting my face. It was stressful but exciting to learn how to plot the radar contact positions of the other ships in company with us and the random contacts of merchant ships we encountered. The trick was to plot them on a paper maneuvering board, or "mo-board" for short, and, using simple geometry plotting the two ships' relative positions and our ship's true course and speed, rapidly calculate the exact solution for the other ship's true course and speed and how closely they would pass us. From that, we could determine what situation existed under the "nautical rules of the road," which would help us ascertain who was privileged (with the right of way) and who was burdened (with the responsibility to maneuver to avoid collision). I'd already learned how to do all that as a midshipman on the Naval Academy's small Yard Patrol (YP) boats out on Chesapeake Bay, but out there it really mattered to get it right. As they say, a collision at sea can ruin your whole day.

Initially, the OOD I was assigned to stand watch with was almost always Lieutenant Junior Grade (LTJG) Pete Coste. Pete was a former enlisted man who had gone to Purdue and earned a commission through a special Navy program to train top notch enlisted sailors with officer potential in engineering. Not only did Pete become a very close friend, but I learned a tremendous amount about seamanship and leadership from him. As the ship's communications division officer, the radio men worked for him, and so did the signal men who stood their watches above us on the signal bridge. It was their job to read and respond to signal flag messages. They were also highly proficient in rapid communications via hand-held semaphore flags and flashing light signals in Morse code. Not surprisingly, Pete himself was really good at flashing lights. As with foreign languages, Morse code is a skill you need to use often to stay fluent, and I had pretty much lost it.

And so, on long, quiet, middle-of-the-night watches, Pete and I would position ourselves on either side of the darkened bridge, where the only lights were the dimly lit indicators from the helm and lee-helm, radar screens, compass and wind indicators, bogey tote board, and navigator's table, all a very faint red to preserve our night vision so we could see the distant lights of ships passing by. From across the bridge, Pete and I would chat for hours in Morse code using the on-off buttons on our flashlights fitted with red filters. Eventually, I got so good at it that, like Pete, I could easily read incoming flashing light messages from other ships, and I would amaze the signal bridge when they called to tell us what the message was. After a signal was received and the signal bridge would call us on the "squawk-box radio" to tell us what the message was, I'd interrupt them and say, "I know… I got it." The confused signal man would again say, "Sir, the message says…" and I'd say again, "No problem, sigs. I read it." I'll always be grateful to Pete for that, and for all the knowledge and experience he shared with me. He was an excellent mentor.

Through our preparations for deployment over the previous six weeks, I had met and gotten to know Pete and all of my fellow officers. But now that we were all limited to the confines of the ship, day and night, and taking all our meals together, I looked forward to getting to know – really know – my fellow members of the wardroom. "Wardroom" is a word used to describe not just the physical compartment on the ship where the officers eat their meals – sometimes called the officers' mess – but it's also the word used to describe the entire group of commissioned and warrant officers assigned to the ship. So, one might correctly, but awkwardly, say, "the wardroom eats their meals in the wardroom."

Let me say a little about being an Ensign, the lowest ranked officer in the wardroom, aside from Warrant Officers, who were in a special category. The best way to describe what was expected of us is to say we were supposed to qualify for watch positions as quickly as possible to become as useful as possible right away, and to let our Chiefs do most of the work of running our divisions. They say "seniority among Ensigns is like virginity among call girls," meaning there isn't any. At that time, it took two years to get promoted from Ensign to Lieutenant Junior Grade (JG), but the promotion was a pretty sure bet if a young officer could walk and chew gum at the same time. But we really did need to do more than walk and chew gum. And there was actually a pecking order of sorts among the Ensigns on *Stoddert.* Traditionally, the most junior of the lot is given the derogatory nickname "George," and the most senior, also measured by date of commissioning, was called the "Bull Ensign." George was usually the guy at the receiving end of a lot of good-natured ribbing, and because of his lowly status, he was supposed to set up the movie projector in the wardroom each night, even if he was too busy to actually stay to watch the movie. The Bull Ensign would wear oversized gold bars on his collars, a tongue-in-cheek way of designating his "special" rank, but otherwise he had no special authority. When I reported aboard, my fellow Ensigns thought they had a new George and joked about this with me at our first lunch in the wardroom. I hadn't said anything about my having already been commissioned for a year, due to my time at graduate school in Monterey and training schools in San Diego, putting me in the middle of the pack in terms of rank among the Ensigns. But, overhearing the conversation, the CO looked up from his meal and said, "You guys had better check his date of rank." When I confirmed I'd actually been an Ensign for fifteen months already, the ribbing stopped cold in an awkward silence. I remember the captain smiling at me.

Bull Ensign Russ Hamm called an "all Ensign meeting" on our first night at sea after leaving Pearl Harbor. Besides Russ and me, the other Ensigns were: my Naval Academy classmate damage control assistant

Jim Moseman, electronic systems officer Jim Farrens, main propulsion officer Roger Wilson, disbursing officer John Brandl, and gunnery officer Dave O'Neil. Some of these guys are still among my best friends over 40 years later.

I showed up for the meeting slightly nauseous and hungry, since I'd skipped dinner in favor of Saltine crackers, the best known (but still insufficient) cure for seasickness. Russ, it seemed, was under the delusion that he had a leadership responsibility for all of us and said something like, "Gentlemen, we Ensigns are going to set a good example and work hard on this deployment. I'm putting out the word right now that for this cruise, we won't watch movies in the wardroom after dinner. If we're not on watch, we'll be studying to qualify for everything as quickly as possible." We all looked at each other uneasily, but nobody said much, with me as the new guy being particularly quiet. But I made two personal vows to myself right then and there: (1) I wouldn't miss a single movie unless I was actually on watch, and (2) I'd qualify at all my watch stations before Russ, who had been on board for several months already. It turns out I came to absolutely love watching movies – a love that continues to this day – and I still managed to do well in my training. Russ was an engineer and stood different watches, so I didn't have the opportunity to compete directly with him in qualifying, and I'm sure he was more than competent. In calling that meeting, I have no doubt he felt he was doing the right thing, but he should have known that we were all pretty depressed at having just left our homes and families for six months. Movies were the only form of recreation we really had. And we were all pretty motivated young professionals who would do our best to qualify at our jobs. At least that's how I felt, while I set about ignoring Russ's moronic "bull orders."

In addition to standing watches in three sections (four hours on, eight hours off, essentially), we were beginning to act like a warship, and that meant preparing for war. Each day, and some nights, in response to the General Quarters alarm and the announcement, "Man your battle stations!" over the ship's 1MC, we would rush to our assigned positions and conduct various drills. These exercises were essential to maintain our preparedness and to keep three hundred and fifty young guys mentally stimulated. They gave us all a clear sense of purpose since this was, after all, a warship.

My newly assigned station was in CIC at the anti-aircraft missile launching console. I found it hard to believe they would give a boot ensign like me the job of actually pulling the trigger which was built into a joystick device that looked like a big dill pickle. (Actually firing a missile was known as "squeezing the pickle," as in "pickling off a missile"). On our third day at sea, we found ourselves off the western coast of Kauai at the Navy's Barking Sands Missile Range. I experienced an intense adrenaline rush when we fired two missiles in an exercise there. On receiving the command "shoot!" I squeezed the pickle, and from two hundred feet astern of me I could hear the muted roar of the TARTAR missile, thrust by its solid rocket propellant, as it literally leapt off the rail and into the sky. What a thrill!

A day later we tied up for a few hours to refuel at Midway Island, a small island at the far northwestern tip of the Hawaiian archipelago. The island, of course, was witness to the tide-turning naval air battle in World War II known as "The Battle of Midway." Besides having a pier for resupplying and refueling Navy ships, Midway was home to a sleepy airbase still used at that time as a training and refueling base by long range P-3C antisubmarine warfare airplanes based at Barber's Point Naval Air Station on Oahu. I knew before arriving that the officer in charge of the Naval Weather Service detachment at the airfield was my graduate school classmate, Lieutenant Charlie Mauck, and it was a great treat to see him when he came aboard the ship to give us a weather briefing. He warned us of a storm brewing ahead, and he wasn't kidding.

Later that same night, underway again and pushing westward, the seas began to rise and the ship's motion became a lot more pronounced. My roommate, disbursing officer John Brandl, came down from standing watch in CIC and said a lot of people up on the bridge and other watch stations were starting to barf. And so, to rise above that challenge, I took my Dramamine, went to sleep and woke up feeling better than I had a right to, which was good, given what the next thirty-six hours would bring.

I remember standing watches on the bridge, watching our bow bury itself in huge waves as a mass of water swept over the entire front end of the ship, engulfing our forward gun mount and torpedo deck, before smashing with great force on the superstructure just beneath the bridge windows. When the ship rolled far over from side to side, if you weren't holding onto something, you were going to be thrown against the bulkhead on one side, and then slide across the bridge to bounce off the other side's bulkhead. The crew was mostly reduced to eating cold sandwiches, if they could eat at all. But once, when we tried to have a sit-down meal in the wardroom, I can recall our navigator LTJG Mike Vanderpool being thrown backward off his chair with a table full of food sliding off the edge after him… and he popped up still holding his plate without having spilled a thing. That was seamanship.

I had been assigned to a two man stateroom, with John Brandl as my roommate. It was located in the forward part of the ship, below decks. I liked the location because I was low in the ship where the motion was less severe and also because I could clearly hear each ping of our sonar coming from a bulbous dome beneath the bow. John and I each had a bunk, he slept in the lower and I (the new guy) had the upper. Each bunk had a metal wire web spring beneath a three inch thick mattress, and each had a reading light at one end. We both had a hanging locker that was probably about ten inches wide, just enough to hang our seldom-used blue dress uniform, a pea-coat called a "reefer," maybe an overcoat (it wasn't required that we own one), and a few items of civilian clothing. All our other clothing items, including our white and khaki uniforms, were neatly folded and stored in a floor-to-ceiling metal chest of drawers, in the middle of which was a fold-down desk top with room inside to store books and paperwork. This was the only place we could display a photo or two of loved ones. Communal sinks, showers, and commodes were down the hall in "the head," which, in those days, still carried the engraved sign on the door "WR & WC," for Wash Room and Water Closet, a carryover from the traditions of the Royal Navy, after which the U.S. Navy had been modeled. Although the two of us were crammed into this small space, we couldn't feel too sorry for ourselves. All of the other officer staterooms were pretty much the same, except for a junior officer four-man bunkroom back aft, affectionately known as Boys Town. Other than Boys Town, each stateroom such as mine was designed for either two officers, or just one in the case of the department heads, the XO, and the CO. Another single occupant cabin was reserved for the squadron commander (called the Commodore) and kept empty except when he was embarked with us as his flagship. The captain, however, had two places to sleep: his relatively spacious stateroom down near the wardroom, and a tiny at-sea cabin just aft of the bridge. For obvious reasons, commanding officers never wanted to be more than a couple of steps from the bridge when the ship was underway, so they spent most of their time sitting on the bridge, sleeping in the at-sea cabin, and only occasionally taking time during the workday below in his cabin to do paperwork, etc.

The XO's room was back on the port side in the after quarter of the ship with several other staterooms, all on one passageway, and just a few doors down the hall from Boys Town. On our third or fourth day at sea, the door to the XO's room went missing sometime during the night. One of my fellow junior officers whose stateroom was near the XO's told me about it, and when I arrived in the wardroom for breakfast, the scowl on the XO's face was my cue to not ask him about the door. In a hushed conversation with another of the junior officers, I learned he had stormed in, mad as hell, as in the middle of the night, when he was away from his stateroom, the door had been removed by an unidentified nocturnal perpetrator. Much quiet mirth was suppressed among all the officers in the wardroom, and yet the XO wasn't saying a word about it to anyone. I had no idea who had taken the door and it's just as well so I had plausible deniability if I was asked.

A word about Lieutenant Commander Parker T. (Pete) Finch, our executive officer, is appropriate here. In face to face conversations, we all addressed him as "XO," as is common practice. (We always called the CO "captain" in our conversations with him, by the way.) But we junior officers, among ourselves, privately referred to him as "Parker T." He also had the secret nickname "Woodstock," based on perceived similarities of appearance to the little yellow bird in *Peanuts* cartoons by Charles Schultz. But such a fanciful nickname was rarely used by us in conversation, "lest a bird of the air hear the matter." The CO called him "Pete," but to everyone else, including the department heads, he was simply "XO." As described earlier, he was not a big man physically, but he had an air of erudite authority which was actually impressive to me. It was easy to tell that he was intellectually brilliant and had a keen ability to keep track of details, skills well suited to the job of executive officer of a ship with over three hundred men aboard. I grew to respect and admire the XO, but he was so much the opposite of our big-boned and big-hearted commanding officer in physique and personality that what (unfortunately) happened was that he became the "bad cop" in most situations, allowing Captain Siegrist to maintain his "good cop" popularity. I'm not proud to say Parker T. often became the target of our junior officer gripes, and sometimes the target of our ill-considered humor.

The "missing door incident" was just such an example of that attempt at humor, which, in truth, was pretty funny. The XO quietly summoned the ship's master at arms, our equivalent of a chief of police among the enlisted men, to discuss the situation. Chief ASROC (antisubmarine rocket) Gunner's Mate Robbie Robinson was well chosen for the job of master at arms. A tall and muscular African American man with a high level black belt in Karate, "Chief Robbie" was the consummate professional, and a little intimidating at first. But he was soft spoken, highly intelligent, perfectly courteous, and unfailingly fair and honest. He was given the job by the XO to "find my door," and it was implied that he ought also to find the person or persons who took it. And so the search of the ship was begun. It was extremely thorough, and yet no "unhinged" door was found. Pretty much all of us assumed it had been thrown overboard. Days went by with the XO living in a stateroom without a door, he using a blanket to cover the entrance. And he still said not a single word about it in the wardroom or, to the best of my knowledge, to anyone on the ship except for Chief Robbie. There were no rants or threats. And there was also no chance in hell that anyone who knew anything about the door would ever tell him, or the chief.

On about the fourth day, the engineering officer was finally told to have his people go ahead and find a little-used door of the same size as the stateroom door, and relocate it to the XO's room, which was done quickly. The next morning, outside the XO's stateroom, leaning against his newly installed door, was *his door!* It took me several weeks to penetrate the secret of who did what and how, and it was well worth the wait. My spilling the beans here may be a true revelation to most of the crew who are reading this, but not to the two perpetrators: my Naval Academy classmate and dear friend Jim Moseman, and our fantastic supply officer, Lieutenant Roger MacInnis. Where had the door been? Jim hid it underneath the three inch thick mattress on his bed. To the best of our knowledge, Chief Robinson hadn't been given authority to search "officer country," although every other inch of the ship from stem to stern and from bilge to mast was searched. The door had been no more than 20 feet away from where it was taken the whole time. And that incident, which most of us thought was hilarious (because it was), made the transit to the other side of the Pacific Ocean just a little bit more fun. I've been told that "door stealing" is a prank that came from the submarine community. Funny stuff.

Our single ship transit to WestPac was a bit unusual for a destroyer in that we didn't deploy with a battle group. Such a group of ships sailing together was most often built around a strike aircraft carrier and would include a mix of cruisers, destroyers, smaller destroyer escorts, and supply ships. Boiler repairs, which had been needed before deployment, had delayed our departure and we wouldn't join company with a battle group until we reached Japan. We did, however, rendezvous in mid-ocean with another group of ships returning home, and with them we conducted maneuvering exercises, which we called "tic-tacs." I'd done similar drills many times on the Academy's Yard Patrol (YP) boats, mentioned earlier. YP's were designed to maneuver like much larger ships, but this was my first experience of controlling the movements of a full-size warship in a formation of ships in the open ocean. The drill involved maneuvering the ship into frequently changing formations which were signaled by flag hoists from a flagship on which a destroyer squadron commander was running the show. Although I was standing bridge watches under instruction, I was using what I'd learned at the Academy about reading signal flags, recognizing station assignment commands, taking bearings to the guide ship, working out the geometry for our required course and speed on a pad of paper maneuvering "mo board" worksheets, and then giving the course and speed orders to the helmsman and lee helmsman. Even though I was doing all this under the watchful and knowing eyes of experienced officers who were responsible for my training, I found myself working independently as a mariner for the first time. It was challenging, exciting, and actually fun!

What was not so thrilling was the daily routine of conducting our internal ship's business, and buckling down to what would be a long deployment that would bring many unknown challenges. As we steamed westward, except for the storm which was well behind us, the transit passed without any remarkable or extraordinarily challenging events. On November 12, we steamed up Tokyo Wan (bay) and tied up at the Japanese/American naval base at Yokosuka. I'd never really succumbed to serious seasickness, even in that heavy weather after leaving Midway Island, but after a long period of time at sea, I stepped ashore and experienced, for the first time, a strange sensation of discomfort. The steadiness of the solid, unmoving ground made me queasy after weeks of compensating for the constant motion of the deck under my feet. But after our trip across the vast expanse of the Pacific Ocean, it was good to be securely tied to a pier again. And it was a blessing to be able to catch up on sleep, the lack of which is about the only guarantee of any naval officer's life at sea.

Before we arrived at Yokosuka, I'd never in my life visited Asia and hadn't lived in Hawaii long enough to become accustomed to its Asian architecture and culture. So Japan greeted me with sights, smells, and tastes that were alien and exciting. In that port, we were guests of the Japanese Maritime Self-Defense Force. Since the end of World War II, the government of Japan has not officially been allowed to have either an army or a navy, although they actually have both in the form of highly professional "defense forces," plus a very competent air force as well. Even though we were visitors, the American presence in Yokosuka was evident, with several ships forward deployed (home-ported) there, including the carrier *Midway* and the cruiser *Reeves.* The base also had an American officers club, and on my first visit to the club, I had the good fortune to run into yet another of my classmates, Ensign John Russell, who was serving on the *Reeves.* John, by the way, had his picture taken while doing a heel-clicking leap off the dais at our Naval Academy graduation, and that picture made the front page of most newspapers in the United States the next day. Today, John is a successful orthopedic surgeon in Florida, but on that day in November, 1974, he was just a fellow junior officer assigned to a warship. He generously invited me to his home that evening for dinner with his wife, Donna, and I gratefully accepted.

On the short trip with John to his off-base housing neighborhood, I commented that I was surprised to see how Japanese residential areas were densely developed and built entirely of wood. And then, inside their small apartment, which was heated solely by a portable kerosene heater, I began to wonder how the Japanese manage to *not* suffer constant and terrible losses to fire. Over the years, though, and right up to the recent disaster caused by the earthquake, tsunami, and fire at the Fukushima nuclear power plant in April, 2011, I learned the Japanese actually do suffer such losses, and always have. I learned during that first visit to Japan, and in subsequent years, how tremendously resourceful the Japanese people are. And I also discovered how friendly they can be if visitors are willing to make an effort to learn about and show respect for their culture. I thoroughly enjoyed the hospitality of my friends John and Donna and the introduction to the country. I loved my first visit to Japan. It set a high expectation for me for all of the adventures ashore that would follow in the coming months.

In today's Navy, most deployed sailors (except those in silent vigil under the seas in our strategic ballistic missile boats), can maintain nearly continuous, or at least frequent, email and social media contact with friends and loved ones at home. Video phone calls via the internet allow children to see their parents and vice versa. But digital words and projected images are a poor substitute for hugs and kisses. The pain of separation is still very much there and tears still flow. In 1974, all we could do was write letters and every now and then, record cassette tapes, and of course wait for letters and tapes – plus the occasional package of badly crumbled home-made cookies or brownies – to arrive in "mail call." And on rare occasions, and at significant cost when we couldn't afford such an expense, we could call home from telephone exchanges at the bases. I learned the phone system quickly but used it sparingly. You would go into the phone exchange, give the operator/manager the phone number you wanted to call and as much cash as you could afford, and get told how many minutes that would buy. You then waited for the call to be placed, and, when they had connected with your number, you'd be waved into a booth with the promise of a one minute warning when the money would run out and the call would abruptly end. The trick was not to spend most of the call crying. In my first ten minute call to Sharon, which cost a small fortune for me as an Ensign, I happily learned Sharon was doing just fine and having fun with Jim Moseman's wife Emily and the other *Stoddert* wives. And she learned I was doing OK, having, if not exactly a lot of *fun,* at least a great experience with the other sailors. And, not surprisingly, we both said how desperately we missed each other. And yes, some of the call was spent letting the tears come – but even that wasn't money wasted.

So there we *Stoddert* sailors were, thousands of miles from home, ready to do our job to maintain the at-peace status of the United States, or ready to go to war if it became necessary. The fact that a war was still going on to our southwest in Vietnam was not lost on us, even though the United States was no longer fighting it. Vietnam seemed distant and not all that relevant to our mission. We more or less knew our mission was simply to provide an American presence in the Asian theater. But we were actually at war – the Cold War with the Soviet Union – and that's what we were constantly thinking about out there.

CHAPTER 5

What's In a Namesake?

BLOODY NEWS. Early this Morning, we were alarmed, with an Express from Newbury-Port, with the following Letter, to the Chairman of the Committee of Correspondence in this Town.

Newbury-Port, April 19, 1775. SIR, This Town has been in a continual Alarm since Mid-day, with Reports of the TROOPS having marched out of Boston to make some Attack in the Country – The Reports in general concur, in part, in having been at Lexington. – And it is very generally said they have been at Concord. – We sent off an Express this Afternoon, who went as far as Simons's at Danvers, before he could get Information that he thought might be depended upon – he there met two or three Gentlemen who affirmed, the Regular *Troops* and our Men had been engaged chief of the Morning, and that it is supposed we had Twenty-five Thousand Men engaged against Four Thousand Regulars; that the Regulars had begun a Retreat...

The New-Hampshire Gazette, Portsmouth NH, April 20, 1775

Going to sea aboard a U.S. Navy ship means becoming part of something special, and sometimes the "special" part derives from living up to some kind of standard implied by your ship's name. Later in my career in the mid 1980s, I served as meteorological officer on the *USS Nimitz (CVN-68).* None of my shipmates on *Nimitz* had any doubt about whose name the ship proudly bore, why our ship's crest was the five stars Fleet Admiral Chester Nimitz wore on his collar, or why he had earned that posthumous honor.

But this is a story about the *USS Benjamin Stoddert.* During that first deployment in 1974, all most of us on the crew knew about our namesake was that he was from Maryland, served as the first Secretary of the Navy, and looked aristocratic in the one portrait we had of him in the wardroom (a copy of what is apparently the *only* image of the man available anywhere). Our ship's logo, printed on all of our "welcome aboard" pamphlets and ship's plaques, etc., was, we were told, the family crest of Mr. Stoddert. One of the duties I volunteered to perform toward the end of my tour on the ship was to make fiberglass molds of the crest, paint them, and mount them on shield-shaped Hawaiian koa wood plaques to be presented to officers departing from the wardroom. I probably made about a dozen of them and, in carefully painting the crest, I always liked the Stoddert family motto the crest carried: "Post Umbra Lux" (After Darkness Light). But maybe because I was just too busy or maybe I was just too lazy, I lacked the curiosity to research who Benjamin Stoddert really was. What I finally found, however, in researching this book, was that Benjamin Stoddert was a significant player in the founding of the United States. And, perhaps more germane to this story, I realized that one could, although it's a bit of a stretch, call him "The Father of the United States Navy."

Such an assertion would baffle, and probably incite to anger, most Navy people who would say, "Whoa, what about John Paul Jones? What about John Barry?" While both of those famous naval officers quasi-officially share that title, Benjamin Stoddert actually deserves consideration as well.

With respect to the Navy's birth, a permanent fog of discord hangs over the city of Salem, or more precisely it's neighboring towns on the north shore of Massachusetts, about twenty miles north of

Boston, as the seagull flies. Setting aside its well-known place in history as the site of the infamous witch trials of 1692, giving it the overly commercialized name "Witch City," Salem has both a good natural harbor and a rich history in the age of sail. As the home port of many commercial ships in our nation's infancy and home to sailors, captains, and now their descendants, the city's heritage is recognized as host of the Salem Maritime National Historic Site. It's also the home of The Marine Society at Salem, which "was founded in 1766 by sea captains to provide relief for disabled and aged members and their families; to promote knowledge of this coast; and to communicate observations for making navigation more safe." Alive and well in this modern age, the Marine Society still holds its quarterly meetings in a small nautical curiosity-filled clubroom, a cabin really, built on the roof of the historic Hawthorne Hotel overlooking Salem Common. Its membership includes descendants of the original Salem sea captains and other distinguished mariners, with one of those descendants and Marine Society members being my wife Sharon!

But the aforementioned fog hanging over Salem comes not just from low clouds of moist air over the sea, although morning fog is common enough there. It's a metaphorical fog for the longstanding, and mostly good natured, argument between its immediate neighboring coastal municipalities, Beverly and Marblehead. Each of these cities – actually a city and a town, respectively – has its own proud place in maritime history and each claims to be the birthplace of the American Navy. Beverly, my boyhood hometown to Salem's immediate north, and Marblehead, my wife's town to its south, have been fighting a running battle of words for many, many years. Those words are sometimes printed on things like tee shirts and sometimes emblazoned on billboards just inside their borders with Salem. For over two centuries, the discord has simmered over which can lay claim to being the birthplace of the

Navy. The billboards and tee shirts say, "Welcome to Beverly, Birthplace of the American Navy," or "Welcome to Marblehead, Birthplace of the American Navy." So, other than this being kind of amusing and interesting to me personally, as a retired Navy officer who hails from one of the claimants and is married to someone on the opposite side, what does this have to do with this story?

The answer comes in the key word in both of those claims: *"American."* While some less-informed enthusiast for his or her hometown may misstate this claim as "Birthplace of the *United States* Navy," the truth is that when the supposed birth of the *American* Navy occurred, there was no country called the United States of America. There were the thirteen British colonies in America, to be sure, and it stands to reason that there had to have been a first time and place that the colonists, under the overall command of General George Washington, took their fight with the British onto the water in an organized fashion, both along the coast and in the major lakes of North America.

Claims aside, here are the facts about the chronology of events. On the evening of April 18, 1775, the red-coated British "regular" troops under the command of General Thomas Gage marched out of Boston on a mission to seize the Americans' arms, ammunition, and supplies in Concord. Their movement was announced by Paul Revere on a night-time ride immortalized by Henry Wadsworth Longfellow's famous poem, and also announced by the two other not-so-well-known riders: William Dawes (a distinguished ancestor in my wife's family) and Dr. Samuel Prescott. The good doctor was the only one of the three who actually made it all the way to Concord. It was the next morning, on April 19, 1775, that the first shots of the Revolutionary War were fired in Lexington. The American colonies, a fledgling nation, were at war with one of the most formidable military powers, both on land and sea, in the world.

Three weeks later, on May 10, Americans under the uncomfortably shared command of the stolid Ethan Allen from Vermont and the charismatic but enigmatic future traitor Benedict Arnold, took the fight to a vital supply line between New England and British Canada on Lake Champlain. Against light defenses, they boldly took Fort Ticonderoga and Crown Point, and shortly afterward took the loyalist settlement at Skenesborough at the southern end of the lake. There, they seized a schooner named *Katherine,* which belonged to a loyalist named Philip Skene. The ship was rechristened by the Americans as the *Liberty* and, under the command of Arnold, she sailed for Saint Johns, Canada at the northern end of the lake. It was near there that *Liberty* engaged and captured the British sloop *Betsy,* which they renamed *Enterprise,* a ship's name that would be oft used for many generations of American warships. These *Enterprises* included America's first nuclear-powered aircraft carrier, one spaceship that never flew in space (NASA's space shuttle for drop/glide/landing tests), and, of course, a series of glorious Federation Starships which have appeared on our small and big screens for fifty years.

It is also worth noting that late in that same month of May, 1775, still just a few weeks after the outbreak of war at Lexington and Concord, the Battle of Chelsea Creek was fought just north of Boston. The Royal Navy's force in Boston Harbor, under the command of Vice Admiral Samuel Graves, sent a contingent of small warships and barges loaded with Royal Marines to engage a sizeable contingent of American militia from Massachusetts, New Hampshire, and Connecticut under the command of Colonel John Stark. Stark had undertaken a bold mission to interdict or destroy British naval stores on Hog and Noodle's Islands, which are now part of modern East Boston. The success of their action denied British access to livestock and hay on the islands but spurred a strong counterattack by the better-armed British naval forces dispatched to interdict them. But the colonists prevailed, capturing and burning the brig *Diana* under the command of Admiral Graves' nephew, Lieutenant Thomas Graves. The *Diana* had run aground trying to withdraw from the creek to open water. That battle, in which the Americans suffered no recorded fatalities while some British sailors and marines were killed, was the first "naval engagement" of the war against the Royal Navy, the first capture of a Royal Navy ship, the first armed action against the British ordered by the Continental Government, and the first battle in which field pieces (cannons) were used by the Americans against the British.

And so, by the end of May, 1775, naval battles with British ships captured or destroyed had been fought by the colonists. An American "navy," with two newly acquired fighting ships, had engaged the enemy on Lake Champlain and taken control of that important waterway, opening a pathway for an attack on the British stronghold in Quebec. And a unified force of American soldiers from multiple colonies (Massachusetts, New Hampshire, and Connecticut) had bloodied the nose of a British Admiral within spyglass range of his flagship in Boston Harbor. But the question is: was an American navy born there on Lake Champlain, or even in the shallows of Chelsea Creek? But wait! There's more.

In the spring and summer of 1775, General Washington didn't have time to think about mounting an invasion of Quebec. He was faced with immediate threats at home from a now very angry superpower. Washington urgently felt the need for a real navy and took first steps to establish one. On September 2, 1775, he commissioned Nicolson Broughton to command the seventy-eight ton, four-gun schooner *Hannah,* which was then owned by relatives of John Glover of Marblehead, a future general who would serve with distinction under Washington. *Hannah's* owners and many of her crew were residents of Marblehead, and no doubt she had spent a lot, or most, of her in-port time anchored snugly in that town's great natural harbor under the protection of Fort Sewell at its mouth. *Hannah* was therefore arguably the first officially commissioned American naval vessel and Marblehead was arguably her home. So Marblehead has a strong case as the Birthplace of the American Navy. But what about Beverly?

In 1775, Beverly was a bigger town than Marblehead, a small city, actually, and with a larger harbor. It was also home to its share of sea captains, sailing ships, shipyards, natural resources, and a thriving maritime industry. And it was from Beverly Harbor that the colonial navy warship *Hannah* was ordered by Washington to put to sea and "cruise against the enemy." Somewhat ingloriously, she set sail from Beverly on September 5, 1775 and was promptly chased into the protection of Gloucester Harbor a little further up the coast by *HMS Lively* and another British ship. After venturing out again a short time later, she was quickly captured by *HMS Unity,* later ran aground on the rocks just off Beverly's craggy coast, and ultimately decommissioned a month later on October 10. So the first commissioned American naval vessel had embarked on its first mission from Beverly. Should Beverly, then, be called the Birthplace of the American Navy? Or should Lake Champlain, Chelsea Creek, Marblehead, or Beverly *ever* be called the Birthplace of the American States Navy, or even referred to as the *United States Navy's* birthplace?

But consider Philadelphia. Representatives at the Continental Congress meeting in Philadelphia had been debating the idea of establishing a navy, given the Brits' overwhelming superiority at sea. On October 3, 1775, the Rhode Island delegates officially put forth a proposal to do just this, but their proposal languished for lack of consensus in Congress. That changed, however, on October 13, when a letter from General Washington was read to the delegates. Washington reported that he had, in fact, taken under his command three small armed ships to intercept British supplies off the Massachusetts coast. Now, having been preempted by their Commander in Chief, the Congress promptly adopted the resolution which was already *de facto* in force, and authorized two additional ships to be outfitted. The American Continental Navy was thus "officially" born, again, a little less than nine months before the signing of the Declaration of Independence on July 4, 1776. And the date the resolution was passed by Congress is as close to official as can be found for the official founding of the Navy. October 13 was authorized in 1972 as the Navy's birthday by Admiral Elmo R. Zumwalt, who was Chief of Naval Operations (CNO) at that time. Thus, the United States Navy celebrates its birthday on October 13 and counts its age in years from that date in 1775. Philadelphia's claim as the birthplace, therefore, would certainly seem to carry weight, even though that city has never produced tee shirts or displayed billboards proclaiming it as the "Birthplace of the American Navy."

On the question of *where* the American Navy was born, then, the answer is a question: who knows? In point of fact, the United States Navy doesn't actually claim a birthplace. I checked every reference book I could find in the Naval Academy library when I was a Midshipman to try to prove my future wife's town was not that birthplace. Of course, I also hoped to prove it was *my* home town. Not surprisingly, I found many references to – backed up by naval history courses I took – the stories of Arnold on Lake Champlain and of the *Hannah* in what was sometimes called "Washington's Navy." But I didn't find reference to a birthplace. At least not an official one. Today, the Naval History and Heritage Command's web site (www.history.navy.mil) addresses this question with just as much ambiguity as I have. Here is what it says:

Because the Continental Navy began in Philadelphia on 13 October 1775, the Navy claims that date as its birthday. A logical corollary would be to recognize Philadelphia as the Navy's birthplace. The Navy, however, also honors the significant naval roles that many other towns played in the American Revolution and does not recognize any as its sole place of origin.

Several localities, in addition to Philadelphia, claim the title "birthplace of the Navy." Machias, Maine, points to the seizing of the Royal Navy schooner *Margaretta* by a small sloop armed with woodsmen on 12 June 1775.

Providence, Rhode Island, asserts its title as the site of the first call for the establishment of a Navy. Beverly and Marblehead, Massachusetts, base their claim on their role in fitting out and manning the small fleet of schooners George Washington employed in the autumn and winter of 1775 to prey on enemy transports. The claim of Whitehall, New York, is based on naval and amphibious operations on Lake Champlain undertaken by the Continental Army under the command of Benedict Arnold. It should be noted that Washington's and Arnold's operations were manned and officered entirely under the authority of the Continental Army. There was no institutional continuity between Washington's or of Arnold's command and the Continental Navy, established as a separate institution by the Continental Congress. The United States Navy considers its beginnings to have been the Continental Navy, not the Continental Army.

Unquestionably the contributions of all of these as well as of other towns to the commencement of naval operations in the American Revolution deserve recognition in any naval history of our country. *Perhaps it would be historically accurate to say that America's Navy had many "birthplaces."*

But regardless of the *place* it happened, the Navy of the United States of America was indeed born. So then, one might wonder who is the *father* of the Navy? This question, rather than the question of the Navy's birthplace, is more germane to this story because there can be only one father of the Navy, right?

Ask almost any naval officer this question, particularly any Naval Academy graduate, and the answer you'll receive will be swift and sure: John Paul Jones. The legendary captain of the Revolutionary War rests with honor in a crypt below the Naval Academy Chapel in Annapolis. His real name at birth in Scotland was John Paul – the Jones was added during his pre-war career as a ship's master in an effort to hide his reputation for cruelty in punishment of his crews. But it was his reputation for boldness and success as a mariner that led to his appointment in December, 1775 as First Lieutenant (second in command) of the 24 gun frigate *Alfred* in the small Continental Navy. A number of significant firsts associated with Jones help support his "paternity" of the Navy. These included the first hoisting of the American ensign over *Alfred,* the newly authorized Continental Navy's maiden cruise in early 1776, and later in 1778 while in command of *Ranger*, the first American vessel to be formerly saluted by another nation, in this case France, after that country formally recognized the new American republic through the Treaty of Alliance between France and America. And in 1779, his *Bon Homme Richard* of 42 guns engaged, and, in a stunning victory, defeated the 50 gun British frigate *Serapis* in a famous naval battle off the coast of England.

Captain Jones never became an Admiral in the Navy of the new United States. After the war, he left America, never to return in his lifetime, and accepted a commission as an Admiral in the Russian Czar's navy. After a brief and unremarkable service there, he spent the remainder of his life doing not much more than drinking in cafes, almost always wearing his Russian Admiral's white uniform. He died and was buried in Paris in 1792. It was not until 1905 that General Horace Porter, U.S. Ambassador to France, took steps to find Jones' humble burial place in Paris and arranged to have his body shipped back to the United States, preserved in alcohol, in a lead casket. Those actions brought Captain Jones to his current resting place in a beautifully designed crypt beneath the Naval Academy chapel. His bold and successful service in a young American Navy is why he is generally revered as a great naval hero, particularly at the Naval Academy. So is this the story of "the Father of the American Navy?" Well, yes and no.

Less well known than the legendary John Paul Jones was Commodore John Barry, who is also widely respected in history and also sometimes credited as "the Father of the American Navy." This claim also has significant merit. Born in Ireland in 1745, Barry also served with distinction in the Continental Navy during the Revolutionary War, having been given command of the 14 gun *Lexington* on December 7, 1775. This was the first commission issued in writing by the Continental Congress. Note, this came after Arnold's victories on Lake Champlain and the commissioning by Washington of *Hannah,* both having happened earlier that same year. While still commanding *Lexington,* he received his captain's commission on March 14, 1776, signed by John Hancock, president of the Continental Congress. He went on to command *Alliance,* in which he fought and won the final naval battle of the Revolutionary War off the coast of Florida. These "firsts" sure seem to make a strong case for Barry's paternity.

John Paul Jones and John Barry were both truly great American naval heroes, and deserve the respect and admiration of those of us who followed them in the naval service of the United States. But these actions were taken in the Continental or American Navy. What about the *United States* Navy? And what about Benjamin Stoddert of Maryland?

Unlike the Scottish and Irish-born Jones and Barry, Stoddert was born in America; Charles County, Maryland to be exact. His father was Thomas Stoddert, a lieutenant in the Maryland militia and hero of the French and Indian Wars. His grandfather was James Stoddert, who emigrated in 1675 from Scotland and became a surveyor in La Plata,

Maryland. Benjamin began his service as a captain in the Pennsylvania Calvary in 1775 and was severely wounded in the September, 1777 Battle of Brandywine Creek, which ended his military career but not his service in defense of his country. After the Revolutionary War, he served as Secretary to the Board of War in the new United States government and resigned in early 1781 to begin a new and highly successful career in mercantile trade from an office just below the fall line of the Potomac River at Georgetown, which, at that time, was within the borders of Maryland.

It was perhaps because of his success as a businessman, perhaps due to his administrative service in the young government, and perhaps due to a personal friendship with President George Washington – or all three – that he was asked by the President to begin discreetly purchasing parcels of land in Maryland, which would become a new "federal city." This land, just east of the Potomac, was mostly an uninhabitable swamp. Today, it's Washington, DC.

John Adams, America's second President, was an ardent federalist who saw his country as a new nation far greater than the sum of its individual states. He was also a New Englander who was concerned about the need to protect American shipping, which he saw as the lifeblood of the country, particularly New England. In post-revolution America, there was no longer much of a fighting navy, and this made United States merchants traveling the vital shipping lanes to, from, and in the Caribbean and the Mediterranean easy pickings for pirates and, even worse, newly aggressive former friends like the French. Adams had little confidence in the management of nautical affairs by his Secretary of War James McHenry, whose department included both the Army the Navy. Early in his presidency, therefore, Adams set out to pull the Navy away from the Department of War and took the matter to Congress, asking for an Authorization Bill to create a Navy Department with its own Secretary to serve on his Cabinet. Because the new department had to be paid for, he also asked for an Appropriation Bill to fund its offices and the growth of its forces.

On May 18, 1798, Adams submitted a request for this legislation and it immediately sailed through both houses. Three days later, the United States Navy was its own federal department and Benjamin Stoddert was confirmed by the Senate as its first Secretary. In celebrating Navy birthdays, May 21, 1798 is little remembered, but maybe it should be.

Secretary Stoddert immediately inherited the previously signed contracts for six later-to-be famous frigates: *Constitution*, *United States*, *Constellation*, *President*, *Congress*, and *Chesapeake*, and for other smaller vessels as well, all of which were in various stages of construction or outfitting. In all, fifty ships were acquired in his first two years of service. He also oversaw the purchase of property to develop the shipyards and docks that later became the Portsmouth Naval Shipyard in New Hampshire, the Boston Naval Shipyard, the New York Naval Shipyard, and the Philadelphia Naval Shipyard. He had to step in with a strong hand to oversee the completion of the ships, assignment of officers, recruitment of crews, and outfitting of a fleet for war. In spite of setbacks and frustrations, he did all these things from his small office in Washington, D.C., the city he had helped to create. And with these ships, he almost singlehandedly (and very capably) managed an undeclared war with France known as the Quasi-War between 1798 and 1801, brought on by murky American-French diplomatic issues and attacks by the French on American shipping, mostly in the Caribbean. After that conflict was resolved, he remained in office well into the first year of the term of the next president, Thomas Jefferson, before resuming his commercial business activities in Georgetown. Benjamin Stoddert, the first Secretary of the Navy and arguably *the Father of the United States Navy*, died on December 13, 1813.

Like others among our founding fathers whose names we should remember but don't, Benjamin Stoddert has two public schools in Maryland named after him and little else. But at least the U.S. Navy had the good sense to name two ships after him: first the *USS Stoddert (DD-302),* a four-stack *Clemson*-class destroyer launched in 1919 and decommissioned in 1933, and, of course, *USS Benjamin Stoddert (DDG-22).*

I highly recommend two books to those who would like to learn more about the founding of the U.S. Navy and Secretary Stoddert: *Six Frigates: The Epic History of the Founding of the U.S. Navy* by Ian W. Toll, and *Stoddert's War: Naval Operations During the Quasi-War with France, 1798-1801* by Michael A. Palmer.

So what's in a namesake? How about the Father of the United States Navy?

PART TWO:
Fun and Games

CHAPTER 6

The Kid Loves Kimchi

Dispatch of the Times, London

PEKING – Without the prospect of any important political breakthrough, four days seems a long time for Secretary of State Henry Kissinger to spend in Peking this week...

There is a strong feeling here that the brilliant coups of Kissinger's early visits to Peking are at an end, and that China and the United States are floundering in the attempt to find a relationship more substantial than the sort of drawing room cordiality that has been established over the past three years...

The areas of conflict between China and the U.S. remain largely unchanged, though they seem to fade more and more into the background of world affairs. Washington continues to support the existing governments in South Vietnam and Cambodia, and China seems unwilling to mediate a solution of the wars in either country.

Also, there appears to be no prospect of serious progress in Korea. Indeed the statement in last year's communique to the effect that China and America should not "negotiate on behalf of third parties" has proved more to the point than either might really have intended.

The main bilateral issue – Taiwan – seems to be frozen for the time being because of its complexity.

Wisconsin State Journal, Madison, WI, November 25, 1974

Secretary of State Henry Kissinger's visit to China was preceded by a visit to Japan, accompanying President Gerald Ford on his first international trip since replacing Richard Nixon in the White House. President Ford's mission was to reassure the Japanese of the close relationship between the two nations. In a November 20 speech, he said the following:

> We believe that we are not just temporary allies; we are permanent friends. We share the same goals – peace, development, stability, and prosperity. These are not only praiseworthy and essential goals but common goals.
>
> The problems of peace and economic well-being are inextricably linked. We believe peace cannot exist without prosperity, prosperity cannot exist without peace, and neither can exist if the great states of the world do not work together to achieve them. We owe this to ourselves, to each other, and to all the Japanese and the American peoples.
>
> America and Japan share the same national pastime – baseball. In the game of baseball, two teams compete. But neither can play without the other, nor without common respect for each other and for the rules of the game.

Our first stop at Yokosuka was to be brief, followed by a voyage to the Republic of Korea (ROK) Navy base at Chinhae. But our visit was actually cut shorter yet when the Seventh Fleet Commander ordered us out of port ahead of schedule because of the President's impending visit. The reason, it was widely believed on board our ship, was that *Stoddert* was configured to carry ASROC antisubmarine rocket-thrown nuclear depth charges, and we were on an operational deployment, so just *maybe* we had "nukes" on board. As part of the standing agreement between the U.S. and Japanese governments, ships that were home-based in Japan, such as the *Midway,* were never allowed to be carrying nuclear weapons while in port. The Japanese were, and still are, justifiably skittish about this particular kind of weapon. Those were among the "rules of the game" President Ford had spoken about. Whether we, as a visiting ship, actually had nuclear weapons on board was classified information, and the assumption had to be that it was possible we were actually armed with them. The official response used by all Navy ships at that time to such queries, was always: "We can neither confirm nor deny the presence of such weapons on board." Under the standing agreements between our governments, this was normally sufficient. But with an American President visiting, this ambiguity wasn't sufficient to ensure the issue of a nuclear-armed ship in a Japanese port wouldn't come up during his state visit. So we cast off and got underway, bound for South Korea. The Koreans couldn't have cared less how we were armed because they lived on a war footing all the time, which was something we soon observed first-hand.

The Chinhae naval base is located in the city of Jinhae-gu, about a three hour drive west of Busan (Pusan) on the Korean peninsula southern coast. The port offered a natural deep harbor surrounded by high jagged mountains. As we approached our anchorage, the entire crew, except those manning positions inside the ship, stood up on deck in our best blue uniforms, shivering in the cold November morning while "manning the rails." We knew the ROKN officers and sailors on their ships and on shore would be scrutinizing our every move since they, themselves, have a highly professional naval service and, as I soon learned, they're very keen to be respected by the U.S. Navy. Captain Siegrist made it clear to my boss Rick Buttina, the weapons officer, who in turn made it *crystal clear* to me as the first lieutenant that we intended to show our respect to the Koreans by making a formal entry into port and to earn their admiration for how we carried it out. We would all be in our dress blue uniforms and we would look sharp in anchoring.

My orders, to be passed on to my division, were that upon arrival, the Bos'n Mates would let go the anchor "smartly" on command, and then the ship's two boats, the captain's gig and the motor whale boat, would be "smartly" lowered to the water from their davits on either side of the ship, landing in the water simultaneously with the anchor being dropped. The boat-docking boom would be "smartly" swung out so the boats could be "smartly" tied up to it. And finally, our accommodation ladder (the removable over-the-side stairway from the main deck to the boats) would be lowered "smartly." That all these things actually did happen perfectly, or so it seemed to my still almost totally untrained eyes, was magical. The Bos'ns and I were awarded a verbal "well done" by both Rick and the captain. Even Chief Spicer had stepped up to the plate and done a great job with the First Division crew.

Getting the crew ashore on liberty from anchorage in those days before today's practice of hiring semi-comfortable ferry boats, was accomplished using our own ship's motor whale boat seating about a dozen men. The captain, XO, and department heads would, of course, be taken back and forth using the gig, which was relatively fast and had a small cabin for comfort and protection from spray. Each boat was manned by a coxswain (doing the steering and engine control) and a boat-hook man, with both drawn from my First Division. There was also an engineman who looked after the diesel engine. If it worked properly, he was just along for the ride. There were times when a "boat officer" was assigned, but normally, the most senior officer who happened to be on the boat for each trip was officially "in charge," meaning if a serious mistake was made, he was responsible, regardless of whether or not he had any control over the situation. The coxswain, then, was a very important guy. As long as he did his job and the boat didn't sink or hit anything, nobody got in trouble. And the Bos'ns from first division, particularly Petty Officers Frankie Taranovich and Mike Lucci, always did a great job.

Liberty for me that day was nothing more than the requisite visit to the small officers' club to consume several adult beverages. There was no phone exchange to try to call home, so top priority was going to be on those beverages. But my fellow officers and I learned we were invited ashore the next day for a friendly tennis match with our ROKN officer counterparts, and we all accepted, assuming more (and hopefully free) adult beverages would be offered.

We showed up at the appointed time on the following day and were a little embarrassed that our tennis clothing options were simply the athletic shorts and tee shirts we had packed for working out onboard ship. Our hosts, though, were all perfectly attired in all-white tennis outfits and it was clear that most of them were very good players who played hard and played to win – every point, if possible. Their good manners at our dismal showing demonstrated what great hosts Koreans are. So we shrugged off our crushing defeat and the embarrassment at our attire and gratefully accepted the food and refreshments we were generously offered.

Our time ashore on this first visit was short because our mission was more than just promoting good will with a friendly country. Allied navies need to be prepared to fight alongside each other, so multinational exercises are common and important. *Benjamin Stoddert* was making this visit to the ROK to take part in just such a bilateral exercise. We weighed anchor the next morning for a joint three day antisubmarine (ASW) exercise called "Tai Kwon Do IV." Shortly after we were underway, I was summoned to the bridge to see Captain Siegrist, who said "Jon, have I got a deal for you." He explained that the Koreans were sending over two young officers to ride *Stoddert* as observers during the exercise. He couldn't afford to send two of our officers in exchange over to them… but he could send me. He explained I was the right guy because I'd already been to Anti-Submarine Warfare (ASW) school in San Diego but wasn't yet the ASW officer, and I wasn't really needed on board because I'd not yet qualified for any watch-standing position. In other words, the message I got was, "You're going because you're expendable." But I ended up taking it as a compliment, particularly as he said I'd be a good ambassador and learn a lot. He didn't say anything about having fun.

Because we were already underway and because neither our ship nor the Korean ship I was being sent to had a helicopter, I was transferred to the *ROKN Ship Chungbuk (DD-95)* in our motor whaleboat, which returned to the *Stoddert* with two young Korean officers. After a quick wave to my shipmates from across the hundred or so feet between us, I was escorted through a watertight door and down several passageways to the stateroom that would be my home for the next three days – a home I wouldn't see much of. As my guide led me through the ship, my senses became alert to the newness of a spoken language and written characters I didn't understand, and a smell unlike any I'd ever encountered. I wouldn't have time to learn the language, but I was determined to find the source of the pungent aroma.

Arriving in "officer country," I was shown into a stateroom, which instead of a door had only a curtain at its entrance. Inside, I was met by my roommate, who very politely introduced himself in tentative but passable English as the ship's doctor. I threw my small bag containing toiletries, a camera, one clean set of khaki uniform shirt and pants, and a jacket on the lower bunk bed; he had moved to the upper one as an act of hospitality.

Without any warning, the curtain was abruptly pulled open with a whoosh, and standing there was an older, stone-faced officer. The doctor leapt to his feet and came to strict attention, and I immediately followed his lead, standing at my very best midshipman plebe summer rigidity. I honestly feared the doctor was about to have heart attack! It turns out that a Korean Navy commanding officer never visits a junior officer's stateroom. But there he was, Captain Kim Jin Gap, stepping into the little room. Ignoring the doctor, Captain Kim stood in front of me and reached out to shake my hand. I had learned in my brief conversation with my roommate that Koreans speaking English have difficulty pronouncing the letter "L" because there's no corresponding sound in their own spoken language. So the captain's heavily accented first words were quickly translated in my mind to, "Ensign Malay, do you play Bridge?" Thank goodness I had figured out this language discrepancy and so replied, "Yes, sir. I know how to play Bridge." He gave me a nod of approval and said, "Good good good. Come." So I grabbed my cap and followed him out the door, leaving the good doctor, whom the captain had not acknowledged in any way, standing at attention with his eyes fixed firmly forward. I'm sure he was relieved to have the room to himself, particularly as I bet that was the first and last visit his commanding officer ever made to his stateroom. In fact, from that moment on I can't really remember ever seeing my roommate again although I did have a couple of brief bouts of sleep in the bunk bed beneath the doctor's over the next three days.

As I followed the captain through the ship, I couldn't help but notice the uniquely pungent smell became even stronger, and I still had no idea what it was.

The *Chungbuk* was actually an American-built destroyer, first commissioned in 1945 as the *USS Chevalier (DD-805).* She was a *Gearing*-class ship built by Bath Iron Works in Maine, operated by the U.S. Navy until she was decommissioned and sold to the South Koreans in July 1972. Her resemblance to the *Stoddert* was mostly limited to only her size and paint color, and I could tell her internal layout of passageways and compartments was quite different from ours. Our walk was short, though, and we soon entered the wardroom, which was similar to the *Stoddert's.* I was surprised to find the room was packed with officers, all of whom, if not already standing, leapt to their feet and to rigid attention as their captain stepped into the room. I had already figured out that senior Korean officers demanded and received tremendous respect – and perhaps fear– from their subordinates.

The captain said something to the officers in their language, no doubt the equivalent of the U.S. Navy term "carry on," meaning "at ease," and the officers relaxed, but nobody sat down yet. He then turned to me and, again in his heavy accent, said, "Ensign Malay. We welcome you to Korean ship *Chungbuk.* Now please teach Bridge!"

I did actually know the basics of how to play Bridge, having a fundamental understanding of the general rules, such as how to bid, play a hand, and score it, but I was no Charles Goren! I had played the incredibly addictive game of Hearts almost every day in my last couple of years in high school, and Pinochle was a staple of my gang at the Naval Academy, so playing cards wasn't foreign to me. But here I was, faced with the challenge of teaching an international audience of men the one game I barely knew.

I sat down with the captain as my partner and two other officers as our opponents, and I began to slowly explain the basics of the game. We played a couple of hands "up" with all cards showing to see how it went, and then a couple of very slow and tentative hands competitively. I had the impression that all the officers not on watch had been summoned to the wardroom for this lesson, and they stood around the table watching and listening carefully. I'm certain some of them could understand very little of what I said, but they politely watched for about twenty minutes or so. Clearly, Captain Kim wanted his officers to learn this "western" game, no doubt based on the same kind of competitiveness demonstrated on the previous day at the tennis courts.

I was feeling pretty stressed, but I knew it would have been very bad manners to display anxiety or irritation in giving this lesson. So I was pleased when the captain pulled the deck together and squared it, put it down, and said, "Good, good! Thank you Ensign Malay. Now, do you want to play a Korean game?" With this, he gave me a genuine smile for the first time. I warmly returned the smile and said, "YES, Sir!" He dismissed all the officers except the two who had been our opponents, one of whom spoke English very well but had up until now said little, except as required to play the game. The captain explained the rules of *their* favorite card game, which they called "No Trump." I was happy to learn any game he wanted to teach me so I could become the enthusiastic student, a much better role than an instructor of a game I didn't know very well to a man who far outranked me.

No Trump turned out to be an enjoyable game, similar to our game of Spades, and easy to learn, particularly if one is already a "teaching professional" at Bridge! It took me a little while to figure out what the Koreans meant when they said "crowbar." But, again, with the "L" issue, they pronounced the suit of clubs as "crowbar." The game was made more fun by my hosts' traditional way of throwing down a winning card by literally slamming it onto the table with a jubilant "ha!" The captain was clearly enjoying himself, and I became more relaxed. We played for about an hour until it was time for the stewards to set up for lunch. I was invited to stay there and found myself chatting for about a half hour with the other junior officer who spoke fluent English while the captain excused himself to attend to his duties, given that his ship was now engaged in a multi-ship exercise. I assumed, incorrectly as it turned out, I would see little of him for the rest of my time on board. The young officer was our equivalent of a Lieutenant (Junior Grade) and his name was Chung Dal-Ho, with Chung being his family name as it was spelled on his name tag. We quickly became Jon and Dal-Ho, and he and I spent most of the next three days together.

While I had met with the captain's favor through my effort to teach his officers Bridge, and for my enthusiastic embrace of their card game, what happened next made me almost a hero with him and the officers of the wardroom. The captain reappeared, and, as the officers prepared to take their preassigned seats around the dining table, he invited me to sit next to him. Lunch service began with white Asian-style rice, which Sharon had in very short order learned to prepare using an electric rice-cooker in Hawaii. She and I still love that style of rice today, referring to it as "sticky rice," which is what everybody in Hawaii calls it. The captain and his executive officer both took healthy servings of rice, and when the bowl was handed to me, I followed their lead and heaped at least two cups of rice on my plate. "A mountain of rice," the CO said with approval. I nodded and smiled.

And then I was introduced to kimchi! I finally discovered the source of mystery pungent smell I had detected earlier. While there were various small and unremarkable portions of meat, fish, and vegetables to be eaten with the rice using chop sticks (which, thankfully, I was already fairly proficient in using), the most important element of the lunch – and, I learned, virtually every Korean meal – was kimchi. This staple in the Korean diet is generally made with sliced cabbage or radishes, scallions, and a seasoned paste of red pepper, garlic, ginger, sugar, fish sauce, salted shrimp, and maybe a little kelp powder. There are variations on the recipe in which other vegetables can be used as well. But kimchi is almost always made with cabbage that has been marinated and then fermented in the spices to the point of limpness until it becomes an intensely spicy and garlicky dish that aggressively assaults both the nose and the tongue. And I was astonished to discover that I loved it! My immediate enjoyment of kimchi both surprised and immensely pleased the captain and the entire table. I think they could tell I wasn't faking it, especially when I asked for a second helping. This scene repeated itself at every meal while I was on board. It was clear they considered me to be quite different from the other Americans they had encountered, most of whom apparently didn't care for kimchi.

So what did I do with my time during those three days at sea? Well, a multi-ship USN/ROKN ASW exercise was going on with sonar searches, maneuvering, flag and radio signaling, etc., and I had been sent to the *Chungbuk* to observe it. How much did I get to observe though? Very little, as it turned out. To my surprise and amusement, I was invited by the captain to play cards with him for hour after hour, often with their destroyer squadron commodore, an even more senior captain who was embarked in *Chungbuk* as his flagship, plus whatever officers could be found to join us. I literally sat in the wardroom playing cards for most of three days, with the game only broken by another meal of rice and kimchi. The captain and I almost became what could pass for friends. I was a very respectful junior friend and he was a very respectable, and sometimes a little scary, senior friend.

I started to wonder who was actually running the ship and its participation in the exercise. Later that first afternoon, during a break from cards, Dal-Ho gave me a tour of the ship. Our first stop was the bridge, where my card game buddy the captain was giving the officer of the deck (OOD) some kind of corrective "guidance." The poor officer looked like he was about to have a stroke. Neither Dal-Ho nor I were acknowledged on the bridge, suggesting we weren't particularly welcome, so we didn't stay long. The bridge is an almost sacred place on a ship at sea, and I was most anxious not to be in the way. Our next stop was the combat information center (CIC) from which an experienced mid-grade officer normally runs the warfighting operations of the ship, like engaging targets with the guns or antisubmarine weapons. He and his team of radar operators; surface, air, and submarine contact plotters; and communications technicians act as the brains of a ship in combat while the bridge provides the eyes and leadership (the OOD, JOOD, and navigation team) for the steering and throttle (the helm and lee helm) to control the ship's course and speed. In actual combat, it's the captain's choice to "fight the ship" from either the bridge or from CIC.

There in CIC, we found a Lieutenant Commander standing over the plotting table on which all the ships of the exercise and other shipping (cargo ships or fishing boats) in the area were being tracked with radar. This type of table had a frosted glass top which was lighted from below and a "dead reckoning tracer," or DRT, a lighted dot that showed the ship's position and moved as the ship moved, with everything marked in pencil on tracing paper taped on top of the glass. From my own training with DRT tables, I was quite impressed with the neatness and precision of the plot the Lieutenant Commander was maintaining. I was also impressed with this officer's command of the situation and the ship's contribution to the exercise. I continued to be impressed with him on each of my subsequent visits to CIC over the three days (during short breaks in our card games). The trouble was that every time I went in there, the same officer was always on duty. I guessed, and Dal-Ho confirmed, that he was the ship's operations officer and the only officer who fully understood the exercise plan and how to operate with the Americans. That guy was at work at that table for almost three straight days, and I sincerely doubt he was able to get more than an hour or two of sleep in that entire time.

Also from my training, I knew that both the American and Korean ships were using a book of signal codes for various communications, such as course, speed, and position orders from the central commander of the combined squadron. This book, the Allied Technical Plan, was always referred to by its acronym ATP-1. It was classified CONFIDENTIAL, the lowest level of security classification, but classified nonetheless. So all orders and reports between ships were being sent using those codes, and I noted the *Chungbuk's* operations officer said on the radio, more than once, the words "bead window." That was a verbal message sent over the radio to all ships alerting everyone that whoever had made the last transmission had committed some kind of error in protecting the security of the code. It's basically a "gotcha," for which the only acceptable answer over the radio was, "Roger, out." And I could tell the Korean officer enjoyed doing it when he could.

At one point during the exercise, however, I noticed a Korean sailor at a table in the corner of CIC with a copy of the code book in front of him talking on the radio very quickly in their language. I asked Dal-Ho what that was all about. He smiled and said, "Ah, that is a Korean circuit." And I got it… the Koreans were probably discussing what the codes meant and what they were supposed to do with other Korean ships over an open (unencrypted) radio circuit. In other words, there was actually zero operational security being exercised, in spite of our Lieutenant Commander's "bead windows!" When I reported this upon my return to the *Stoddert,* Eric Utegaard, our own operations officer, told me he was aware of this, and we were perfectly OK with it because it was a common practice. What was important, he said, was the development of U.S.-ROK warfighting skills and experience in working together. That's what the exercise was all about.

Dal-Ho was at one of the seats at the card game for much of the time I played. The captain, the commodore, the doctor, and the operations officer I had seen in CIC all spoke English quite well, but Dal-Ho was unique because of his command of the language. Curious, I privately asked him what job he had on board that allowed him time to play cards and hang around with me, he being a LTJG, only one step above my own rank of Ensign. He said he was responsible for "public affairs," and later I began to figure out this could also be construed as "political affairs." He said his fluency in English was why he was "detailed" to host me, but I couldn't help but suspect I was considered a potential source for intelligence leaks regarding my ship and U.S. Navy operations. Fortunately, I was able to compartmentalize that probably unjustified concern, carefully watch what I said, and still get to know him as an extremely intelligent and interesting person, and as a new friend.

On our second day at sea, the captain was called away from our card game, and he indicated I should follow him. Arriving topside, I saw the *Chungbuk* had ordered a small (fifty feet or so in length) fishing boat to heave to and come alongside. I was fascinated to see our ship had stationed several men with rifles and battle helmets along the topside rails and they were all aiming down into the fishing boat. An armed boarding crew went aboard her while the fishermen stood in view with their hands in the air. Our ship's men did a quick but efficient search of the boat, and finding no contraband, it was soon released and our crew stood down. A *de facto* state of war between North and South Korea existed then, and still does today, with only a tenuous ceasefire maintaining relative peace since the Korean Armistice Agreement was signed on July 27, 1953. Because of this, searches of suspicious boats were routine back in 1974, and still are today. I was impressed with the deadly seriousness of what I had witnessed. *Chungbuk* had broken away from the exercise to conduct this interdiction, but as soon as it was over, it was back to ASW for the ship, and back to cards and kimchi for me. As the expression goes, it was a job and somebody had to do it!

The exercise ended in the early afternoon of the third day, and I was excited about returning to the *Benjamin Stoddert.* Not only was I thinking about coming off my diet of rice and kimchi, but I was anxious to have dinner with my shipmates because it was Thursday, November 28 and Thanksgiving Day. I knew my ship's wardroom cooks – and the crew's mess deck cooks – had all the fixings to make a traditional "turkey day" dinner. Alas, however, there was no turkey for me that day.

I was informed that *Chungbuk* was returning to port, and *Stoddert* had indicated it would stay at sea until the next morning so the crew could celebrate the holiday. I guess Captain Siegrist didn't want the crew to have to choose between getting drunk in town and having a turkey dinner! Little did I know my Korean adventure was going to take a new direction.

After tying up to the pier in the late afternoon, I said goodbye to Captain Kim and thanked him for his warm hospitality and went ashore. I checked into a room at the small American compound's bachelor officers quarters (BOQ) which was only a short walk from the piers. These lodging facilities, fixtures on U.S. military bases everywhere, are essentially no-frills hotels for visiting officers and senior civilian government employees, and they're generally located next to, or part of, an officers club. Chinhae was the headquarters for the U.S. Navy's advisory group to the Korean Navy, and so had both a small BOQ and officers club. I had an early dinner of a cheeseburger and fries at the club, with neither kimchee nor turkey being an option.

I had made plans to meet Dal-Ho that evening at an off-base coffee house, and he had written the name of it in Korean for me to show to a cab driver, and its name spelled out phonetically in western characters for me to pronounce. Leaving the base, I felt self-conscious in my khaki uniform and lightweight cotton military jacket, wishing I could blend into the city in civilian clothes – but I'd not been allowed to bring them to the *Chungbuk* with me. I hailed a cab and set off into yet another new and exotic world. It was immediately evident that the town of Jinhae-gu was very different from Yokosuka, Japan: different in sights, sounds, and smells.

Despite showing the cab driver the coffee house's name and doing my best to pronounce it as I'd been taught by Dal-Ho, it took the driver three attempts to find the place. I guessed that was he was simply driving to random coffee houses, assuming this dumb American wouldn't care which one he went to. But on the third try, I confirmed with people at the door this was indeed the right place, paid the taxi driver (who was very happy to take my U.S. dollars), and went inside. Dal-Ho was there already, still in his working uniform, wearing the standard dark blue nylon jacket with a fur collar that all their officers wore. I remember being jealous of his jacket because it was pretty chilly outside and the ROKN blue jackets looked both very warm and very "cool," as seventies fashion went.

My new friend explained that the reason he enjoyed this particular coffee house was that they played only classical music – mostly European, but Korean as well. He also told me he was an admirer of the arts, and the place's owner was an excellent impressionist artist and art teacher. It was quiet and pleasant, and I surprised Dal-Ho with my ability to identify some of the western composers I heard and also to name the different styles of art displayed on the walls, like the cubist and abstractionist work of Paul Klee, who I truthfully said was one of my favorite artists. Because we were both tired, we only drank a bottle or two of the popular Korean beer called OB, for Oriental Beer. I liked it very much and truly enjoyed the company. As we said good night, he presented me with a rolled up piece of thin rice paper on which was a delicate red and black watercolor of tree branches and blossoms with the signature "chop" of the artist. It was magnificent in its beauty and simplicity. I was deeply touched when he told me it had been painted by his girlfriend, and he could tell I was genuinely grateful for such a personal gift. He invited me back to the same place the following evening so he could introduce me to her and show me some traditional Korean hospitality and culture. I gratefully accepted. My taxi ride back to the base was uneventful, and my night's sleep in the BOQ was glorious.

The next morning, I stood on the pier as *Stoddert* anchored and went quickly aboard the first boat coming in so I could report back aboard. Because the captain had just left to go ashore on the gig, I immediately sought out the XO and gave him a debriefing of my time on the *Chungbuk*. I'm sure I downplayed the card playing and talked instead about my tours of the ship. We both thought it was odd that my orientation tour of the ship never included their SONAR room or any of the engineering compartments. He was amused to hear the story of the single Lieutenant Commander at the DRT table for the entire three days and confided, "We thought we were detecting the same voice on the radio for almost the whole exercise." He thanked me for being a good sport and told me the two young Korean officers who had ridden *Stoddert*, Ensigns like myself, had been very shy, kept to themselves, and took little interest in what was going on. He also said they spoke little English, which may explain their shyness – and I suspected my shipmates hadn't done very much to be warm to them since everybody on a U.S. Navy warship is always extremely busy and exhausted. I'm sure it would have been a better experience for those guys if my ship had assigned an officer to be their host, as Dal Ho had been for me.

That evening, I went ashore in civilian clothes and found the same coffee house, which was much easier this time. Dal-Ho, also in civvies, met me there and introduced me to his girlfriend, whose name was Jeen Sung-Hee. She was shy, delicate, and pretty, and it became obvious the two of them were truly in love, and they said they were planning to be married. To return Dal-Ho's kindness for the painting, I'd gone to the small Navy Exchange store on the U.S. compound before leaving the base and bought several pouches of different flavors of pipe tobacco for him. I remember him smoking a pipe as we played cards and hearing him say it was virtually impossible to get western-style pipe tobacco, or even good pipes, in South Korea. I suspected it may not have been legal for me to buy and transfer tobacco from the American-run store to a

Korean, but it was a gift and not purchased for him with his money, so I convinced myself it was OK. He was deeply touched by the gift and confirmed I'd taken a chance in bringing the stuff off the base for him. For the rest of the evening, he treated me like an honored guest.

First we went upstairs to meet the coffee house's owner, the artist whose work adorned the walls, to discuss art with him. He told me he taught pre-university art students classical techniques, copying Raphael, Greek statuary, and the impressionists. His own works on display were impressive, but he said he refused to sell them because "the rich Koreans who would buy them wouldn't make an attempt to understand the thought behind them." He said he was happy with his coffee shop and his teaching. Then he dropped the subject and proudly showed off his collection of Korean antiques, one of which was a stone vase a thousand years old. What an interesting gentleman!

I wrote the following description of the evening to to Sharon the next morning – when I was quite hung over.

Going back downstairs, Dal-Ho and his lady introduced me to three different hot teas, or cha, which I enjoyed and bought a package of one of them to take home with me. Saying good night to Sung-Hee, he and I walked to a small and dingy bar nearby, a place no American would likely notice or be interested in. But once there, he treated me to a great meal and spirits. For food, we began with raw oysters and mussels served with a hot tomato sauce which were delicious. I enjoyed them, but with no small amount of apprehension. But I knew I had to trust his judgment as to the safety of the raw seafood, correctly recognizing he was a gentleman who would never do anything to get me sick. We then had a plate of fried shrimp – very delicious and tender; then bin tae tuck (spelling this phonetically), a pastry to dip in soy sauce, and again excellent. For drinks, we each began with a couple of bottles of OB and then moved on to small glasses of soju, a colorless Korean liquor distilled from potatoes. It was clearly very potent and I knew we were happily heading down the path to getting very drunk. But before I lost my taste buds, he introduced me to the most traditional of Korean drinks: makkoli (also sometimes spelled makgeolli or makgoli), a milky and sweet white rice wine served to us in bowls. I loved it! We then moved on to Korean sake, served with a fish fin floating on top which gave it a very pungent odor and taste. Everything was exotic, delicious, and we had clearly become pretty tipsy.

Leaving the bar, Dal-Ho pointed out it was very late and said there was a very, emphasizing VERY, strict curfew. I followed his lead when he began to run... and then run faster. Had we been able to see and run straight, we might have made the trip back to the Navy base more quickly, but we passed the stone-faced guards at only a minute or two before midnight and the start of curfew. We caught our breath, gave each other hearty handshakes, and said we hoped our paths would someday cross again.

I never saw Dal-Ho again after that evening since *Stoddert* got underway the next morning. From time to time over the years, I wondered what kind of career path he had followed, but I was confident he was likely a very big success in whatever it may have been. Happily, through a very simple online search, I found this update on my card-playing, pipe-smoking, music- and art-admiring friend.

> Ambassador Dal-Ho Chung graduated from Seoul National Univ. in 1971, majoring in Political Science. He continued his study at the SNU Graduate School for one year before entering military service with the Korean Navy (1972-1975). As he began his career as diplomat, he joined the Foreign Service Program of Oxford University (1977-1978). While working in New York, he studied at NYU (1988-1990), where he obtained his M.A. in International Politics. He also became a Fellow of the Harvard University's Center for International Affairs (1996-1997).
>
> In his diplomatic carrier spanning thirty-three years, he served as Ambassador to Panama (2002-2004), Ambassador at Large for Korean Nationals in Foreign

> Countries (2005-2006), and Ambassador to Egypt (2006-2009). Previously, he served in different countries with different positions - Austria, France, New York (ROK Mission to the United Nations), Iraq, and Norway. He also served as Director-General for International Organizations, Deputy Assistant Minister for Planning and Budget, and Director for UN Affairs at the Ministry of Foreign Affairs.
>
> Since Jan. 2010 he serves as Executive Director of CIFAL Jeju. Since April 2012 he serves as Chairman of the Foreign Advisory Committee for the Governor of Jeju Special Self-Governing Province.
>
> *From: United Nations Institute for Training and Research web site*

Although I corresponded with Dal-Ho a few times in the months following those exciting days in South Korea, eventually one or the other of us stopped writing as we moved on with our lives. However, in discovering his extremely distinguished resume while writing this book, I also found an email address and we established a new connection. I learned from him that his lady friend Jeen Sung-Hee had become, and remains, Mrs. Chung Sung-Hee, they having married in 1975. I learned she had continued to develop her talents as an artist and had several exhibits during their time stationed in a diplomatic assignment in Vienna.

Also, by the way, Captain Kim, my card-playing friend, went on to become *Admiral* Kim. And as for me, I still love sticky rice and kimchi, and I don't believe I've ever again played another hand of Bridge since that day in the wardroom of the *ROK Navy Ship Chungbuk*!

CHAPTER 7

Land of the Rising Sun

SAIGON (UPI) – South Vietnam's air force pilots Saturday claimed killing more than 60 Communist soldiers in strikes on North Vietnamese strongholds as both sides predicted heavy fighting for control of the country's new rice harvest.

In Phnom Penh, Cambodian President Lon Nol issued a fourth call for peace talks with Communist insurgents of exiled Prince Norodom Sinhanouk, two days after the U.N. General Assembly voted to continue seating the incumbent Phnom Penh government in the world body.

The Saigon command said its pilots killed 47 Communists in air strikes Friday against North Vietnamese strongholds around the government's Rach Bap militia base 20miles north of Saigon. Other air attacks on Communist positions below the demilitarized zone and in the Mekong Delta killed 14 Communists.

The Viet Cong accused the government of President Nguyen Van Thieu of planning "to destroy the rice of the people" and warned of "punitive actions against Thieu's troops if destruction of the rice crop is not stopped."

The Port Arthur News, Port Arthur, Texas, Sunday, December 1, 1974

Vietnam remained far to our south, and far from our thoughts. And back home, stories like the one quoted above were deeply buried in our home town newspapers. Although not very often on the front page, news from Vietnam was still making it into the press, and we were able to follow war stories through the news service clippings we would periodically receive on the ship. But our thoughts weren't on the war – a war we weren't fighting – but rather they were on our families and on our next two destinations, both Japanese port visits. December arrived as we departed from Korean waters en route back to Japan, this time to the naval base of Sasebo on Kyushu, the country's southernmost major island. Sasebo was once Japan's major naval base, having been established when the site was selected by Admiral Tojo of the Imperial Navy before World War II because of its strategic location just 130 nautical miles across the Tsushima Strait from South Korea's base at Chinhae and the nearby city of Busan. Sasebo, blessed with a very large and deep harbor, is about 30 miles northwest of the city of Nagasaki and had been host to a U.S. Navy facility since the end of the war. That base was still in operation when we visited. It was the headquarters of the Commander of the U.S. Seventh Fleet and home port for his flagship, the guided missile cruiser *USS Oklahoma City (CLG-5).*

Our transit across the strait was relatively short and we were soon at "Sea and Anchor Detail" steaming up the channel toward our pier-side berth. This was to be our crew's first real R&R stop and the anticipation throughout the ship was huge since our first visit at Yokosuka had been brief and busy and at Chinhae we had anchored out, which kept many of the crew on board. I knew this stop would be very enjoyable.

Captain Siegrist set the tone for me, as I recall. We were steaming up the channel to the base and both he and I were on the port side bridge wing, watching the nearby shoreline slip past. I wasn't standing watch since I was still vastly underqualified to serve on the navigation detail on the bridge. But the captain didn't mind, and in fact encouraged, junior officers to come up to the bridge during maneuvering situations to observe and learn, just so long as we stayed out of the way. So I found myself having sort of a "father and son" moment with the captain out in the open air of the bridge wing. Pointing to a hill just coming up off our beam, he said, "That, Jon, is what we call Jane Russell Hill." It took me only a couple of seconds to figure out what he meant, remembering the physical attributes which had helped make that popular starlet of the 1940's and 50's become famous for more than her acting. I later learned the nickname for the hill was well known to the Navy and I can imagine old salts (like my CO) pointing it out to young salts (like me) for many years. I doubt it's still happening today because it's a sure bet that none of today's young sailors (or even their commanding officers) have ever seen a movie starring Jane Russell. And it's a healthy thing that sexist stuff like this is fading into the past.

I mention this port visit, which was otherwise pretty unremarkable, not just for a hill we passed while navigating to our berth, but also for the other thing that port was known for; the officers club's Monkey Bar, which had caged monkeys behind the bartenders. Cold beverages and free entertainment – they were both very welcome and memorable!

We enjoyed a three day stop there, time enough for every member of the crew to get two days of quality time on liberty ashore. This meant there was a chance for them to pursue what sailors generally want: alcohol and women, usually in that order. I think I slept through most of the time in port, but one other thing I do remember was this being my first opportunity to visit a couple of "sailor bars" and watch American sailors in full pursuit of traditional liberty activities. I didn't yet know that what I saw in Sasebo paled in comparison with what awaited us in just a few weeks at Subic Bay in the Philippines, but it was still a sight to behold. Our crew was actually on relatively good behavior because of three factors: first was the traditional reserve of the Japanese personality, reflected even in the ladies trawling the bars, even though it was their job to separate the sailors from their dollars; second, the crew had been sternly warned by the captain to be on good behavior because of unruly sailor behavior during other ships' recent visits and our conspicuousness after President Ford's recent visit; and third, it was still early in the cruise.

Our Japanese experience continued after another short time at sea, ending once again tied to a pier at Yokosuka on about the 7th of December, or "Pearl Harbor Day," which was certainly an interesting time for reflection on the U.S.-Japanese partnership in sharing naval repair facilities. It was on this visit that I witnessed another element of Japanese culture as it applied to visiting ships: Yokosuka had an excellent work force of highly skilled and hardworking shipyard workers whose services were contracted for by the U.S. Navy. Almost immediately after our arrival, they swarmed aboard and set to work on repairs I hardly knew we needed. Across the piers, we could see the aircraft carrier *USS Midway (CV-43),* which had long since been "forward deployed" to Yokosuka, meaning that base was her full time home port. I learned she literally could not be returned home to the States for continued service because she had been in Japan so long that all of her ship's drawings for any future shipyard work were now annotated in Japanese! And, in fact, *Midway* never did come home until she was decommissioned. She now sits tied to a pier as a floating museum in San Diego, California.

Unlike our relaxing liberty visit to Sasebo, this visit to "Yoko," as we called the base, was mostly to get work done, but with a little pleasure mixed in. The base had an excellent officers club – institutions which, sadly, are now almost completely gone from U.S. Navy bases in the States and around the world. But in 1974, O' Clubs were the "go-to place" for officers, just as the Enlisted and Chiefs Clubs were popular with the crew. I have happy memories of my frequent visit to the O' Club in Yoko for liquid refreshment and meals, and at the strong recommendations of those who had been there before, I went one time for a "hotsie bath" in its basement. The traditional Japanese hot tub bath that the club offered as one of its services was presided over by a tiny, elderly Japanese lady who would prepare the tub then entertain her clients by playing the harmonica for them while they soaked. I was surprised by her extensive repertoire of Christmas music!

A visit to the American Navy Exchange store on the base also provided a memorable experience. Buyers for this Exchange had acquired a vast assortment of Asian furniture, artwork, electronics, toys, clothing, etc., and make everything available for sale, tax-free, at incredibly low prices. You could go out into the local economy and shop by haggling to get to a price (something inexperienced Americans are notoriously lousy at doing) and buy many of the same items that were found at the Exchange. But why? Walking through the store, I was entranced by the wonders I could bring home. To this day, I'm proud of my purchases; two tall brass and green marble lamps.

Before we left Yokosuka, our wardroom was invited to a holiday party at the on-base home of Commander Rudy Daus, the commanding officer of the *USS Parsons (DDG-15).* His ship was a destroyer in the same class as *Stoddert,* and, like the *Midway* and the *Reeves,* was stationed there. He and his wife generously provided a large spread of food and an open bar, which I enjoyed with everyone else. I was still in fairly good shape until our host, in celebration of the holiday spirit and his Russian heritage, began the vodka toasts. As he broke out several bottles from his freezer, shot glasses were handed out to everyone. Each of the impressive series of toasts, which I quickly stopped counting, ended with the singing of an honorarium to Czar Nicholas II: "Nicolashka, Nicolashka, Nicolashka Nicolai. Nicolai, Nicolai," and ended with a shouted "Nostrovia!" to which we drank. As soon as the shots were downed, another round was quickly poured! That night I was more than happy to join our host as a Russian, at least until everything became a blur. I'm lucky someone remembered where we were, because

I woke up in my rack the next morning back on the ship. And to my fuzzy memory of that evening, all I can say is "Nostrovia!"

The Christmas spirit having set in that night, we soon set off again for the port where we would actually spend December 25, the city of Kaohsiung in the Republic of China on Taiwan.

CHAPTER 8

Christmas Presence

By Charles R. Smith, UPI Senior Editor

HONG KONG (UPI) – American military ties with Taiwan still stand on a solid foundation with no sign of significant erosion in the immediate future.

Except for a troop cutback that is part of a general reduction of U.S. forces in Asia, there has been no basic change in U.S. military relations with Taiwan since former President Richard M. Nixon's visit to China in 1972.

When President Ford recently signed a bill repealing a congressional resolution authorizing the President to intervene militarily in defense of Taiwan some saw it as a move of considerable significance.

The action was far more form than substance. It really changed nothing in terms of U.S.-Taiwan military relations. It merely wiped off the books an almost 20 year old outdated resolution applying to another time and a radically different situation.

The Daily Herald, Provo, Utah, Wednesday, December 25, 1974

The port city of Kaohsiung is on the southwestern coast of the island nation of Taiwan, about 350 nautical miles due east of Hong Kong, and only half that distance to the nearest point on the Chinese mainland coast across the Taiwan Strait. Its large harbor is home to the Republic of China Navy and its Naval Academy. It promised to be an interesting place to celebrate Christmas, but first we had to get into the harbor.

We steamed toward the port, and from a distance we could see the harbor was extremely busy and crowded. Our radar showed hundreds of vessels near the entrance to the inner harbor, a very narrow passage between the ends of two long stone breakwaters coming out from the shore to the north and a sliver of an island to the south of the entrance. As we approached, we crept along in a tangle of large and small ships heading in, while another group of ships was trying to come out, with all of us vying for the right-of-way to pass through an opening only about 450 yards across, which is just a little wider than a modern supertankers is long. The only protocol seemed to be that, at least in the narrow channel itself, the "port to port" crossing rule was being followed, with ships staying to their right hand side of the shared opening. But both outside and inside the channel, it was utter chaos.

Captain Siegrist had nerves of steel and our operations officer Eric Utegaard was an extremely competent officer of the deck for these tricky "sea and anchor detail" situations. It was my impression that they simply pointed the sharp end of our ship toward the entrance and moved relentlessly toward it with minimum dodging and weaving, hoping other ships and boats would simply get out of the way. As one might suspect, large gray warships actually do get some respect, and we managed to sail through and onward to our anchorage without incident. I had already developed a huge admiration for Captain Siegrist for his skillful ship handling, but getting into Kaohsiung that day moved him up another notch.

During liberty ashore, in my very few visits to "sailor bars" near the port, I quickly found that the restraint I'd seen in our sailors' behavior in Japan wasn't required in this town. Since this new scene wasn't my cup of tea, I set my priorities instead on enjoying the culture and sights as best I could. There were some beautiful parks, one of which featured a wonderful bridge which zig-zagged across a serene pond to an island garden – the many turns on the bridge symbolically keeping evil spirits from passing across. Who knew that evil spirits had such a wide corner turning radius?

There was, however, a cab ride in which "evil spirits" paid me a visit. Roger Wilson, my fellow Ensign, who was eventually to relieve me as first lieutenant, was assigned to the engineering department and we were in a taxi when our non-English speaking taxi driver pulled over and bought something from a roadside vendor. It was a paper cone filled with what appeared to be some kind of nut, and he immediately popped a few into his mouth. With a grin that was eerily colored by something bright red coating his teeth, he turned around and held the cone to us, clearing offering us a taste. Not making the connection between that strange red mouth and the nuts, Roger and I assumed this was nothing more than a local snack, so we accepted and each popped a couple of nuts into our mouths. With my first bite down on them, I was hit with an extremely bitter, unpleasant taste and immediately spit them out into a handkerchief. Roger, a little more adventurous than I, continued chewing. In about a minute, I developed a slight lightheadedness, not unlike my few prior experiences with chewing tobacco. I began to suspect these weren't snacking nuts, and I looked over at Roger. His teeth had turned bright red like the driver's, and he told me he was pretty well buzzed. We later learned we'd had the "pleasure" of experiencing the chewing of areca nuts, which are commonly referred to as betel nuts. A "mild stimulant," they produce an effect similar to the chewing of betel leaves. I now know the chewing of both areca nuts and betel leaves is commonly practiced in Asia. The red stains in our mouths didn't last long and Roger slowly came down from a sensation he later described as akin to very quickly drinking about ten cups of dark coffee.

On a happier note, we discovered Taiwan's cuisine was spicy, rich, savory, and quite delicious, and it was unlike what I'd experienced in

Chinese restaurants stateside. Accordingly, I took advantage of several opportunities to dine ashore, enjoying each meal immensely. But there were, of course, still things to be taken care of back on the ship and watches to be stood. And, being cash poor, shipboard free meals also had their appeal. One afternoon, I was returning to the ship for dinner. As we approached the ship, which was riding at a mooring buoy in the center of the harbor, I was surprised to see about two dozen Asian men, not dressed in the Navy dungarees and white tee shirts our men would have been wearing, but in all kinds of dress, sitting or standing on planks suspended from the deck. They were busy painting the sides of the ship. Others were on bamboo ladders, painting the superstructure topside. I reminded myself that, as first lieutenant, I was responsible for the preservation and appearance of our ship's exterior surfaces and so, scurrying up the ladder from the boat, I rushed to the fantail (the exterior main deck furthest aft where our after gun mount was located) and found Bos'n Silva pouring five gallon cans of haze gray paint into a fifty-five gallon steel drum and stirring it with a broomstick.

"What the hell's going on, Boats?" was all I could manage to say. Silva smiled at me in his huge Hawaiian good natured way and said "No worry, Mr. Malay. We're just painting the ship."

"I can see that," I said. But how the (expletive) are we paying for all these (Chinese) guys?"

"Oh, don't worry about that, sir. It's taken care of."

"Does the captain know?" I blurted out.

"Oh, yes sir. He OK'ed it."

And the schooling of Ensign Malay continued with another lesson learned. Silva had waited for me to go ashore (giving me plausible deniability, I suspect), jumped several levels of the chain of command and went directly to our experienced-in-the-ways-of-the-old-navy-world captain (giving him top cover). He explained how, through a local agent he knew from past visits, he had arranged and "paid for" this labor force of about 25 local workers called stevedores by simply allowing the agent to arrange to pick up our trash, to which Silva had added a few extra things he had squirreled away, including an old mooring line and a couple of old beat-up brass boat propellers. We already had plenty of gray paint in our store rooms, ready for our crew to use when the opportunity permitted. There in Kaohsiung, for the price of giving away our trash and other excess stuff, we had a beautifully repainted ship which, for the next couple of months, looked far better than other Navy ships with which we were in company. Because it had all been done at one time using the trick of mixing the five gallon cans of paint together, there would be no seams visible between different cans with slightly different shades of gray, as was usually the case. The captain, familiar with these highly practical work-arounds in foreign ports, was fine with it. The other officers between the CO and me, namely the XO and my department head Rick Buttina, were quiet on the subject, no doubt in deference to the captain and admiration for our three hundred pound Hawaiian Bos'n. And, of course, both the XO and Rick, plus our supply officer Lieutenant Roger MacInnis who supplied the paint, were all experienced WestPac sailors and knew this was the way business was done out there. And I had learned something new.

Sharon was thousands of miles away and I missed her terribly, even more so because it was Christmas. But the very welcome letters from her that were delivered to the ship, our expert paint job, and a thoroughly enjoyable port visit, were all pretty good Christmas presents.

CHAPTER 9

Subic Special

SAIGON (UPI) – President Nguyen Van Thieu predicted a gloomy year today for South Vietnam. At about the same time Communist forces captured the last military headquarters in Phuoc Long province and threatened the province capital.

In a speech to the military, Thieu said, "You as well as I do not believe that the Communists will answer our call to return to serious bargaining between now and Tet (the oriental New Year, Feb. 11) to implement the cease-fire in an acceptable way."

The Daily Herald, Provo Utah, Wednesday, January 1, 1975

South Vietnam's president was prescient in predicting a gloomy 1975. But as history soon revealed, gloomy was a gross understatement. For the *Benjamin Stoddert* crew, 1975 held the prospect for less than a half year of gloom, to be followed by our planned homecoming in late May, and shortly thereafter entering the Pearl Harbor Naval Shipyard for a full year in overhaul. Overhauls meant dirty and demanding work for the ship's force, but they also meant only about half the normal rotation of duty days spent working all day and sleeping on board or in a berthing barge alongside. And that, in turn, meant most nights and weekends could be spent at home with our families, enjoying Oahu beaches, and the other islands as well. We could also look forward to hosting visits from our mainland families and friends. In short, life would be much more fun when we got home than it was out there, since we'd be coming home to paradise.

Far from paradise, but not without its own attractions and fun, the U.S. Naval Base at Subic Bay was our next stop. Now long closed as an American-controlled facility and booming today as a commercial shipping and tourism center for the Philippine government, Subic is located on the west coast of the island of Luzon, about sixty miles northwest of the much larger Manila Bay. Because of the special relationship that had existed between the United States and the government of the Philippines since World War II, the U.S. was allowed to build a sprawling base at Subic that included ship piers, a shipyard, and the adjacent Cubi Point Naval Air Station. This naval complex had been the epicenter of the massive resupply and repair activities of the U.S. Seventh Fleet during the Vietnam War. With ships such as ours still maintaining American military presence in the theater, it was still a bustling Seventh Fleet port when we arrived for our first visit just before New Year's Day, 1975. The base was strategically located, and it was relatively inexpensive compared to maintaining facilities and operating shipyards in Japan or other WestPac ports. And it was the ultimate "sailor playground." We correctly suspected we were about to start seeing a lot of Subic Bay and its adjacent Olongapo City.

Not far from the destroyer piers at the base, there was a mini officers club called the Chuck Wagon. They served up a tall, red, fruity, potent, and dirt cheap tropical drink called the "Subic Special," and it's easy to use that drink's name as a metaphor for the whole Subic experience. Having been coached by shipmates who were old hands at Subic Bay visits, my first Subic Special and their reportedly very good American-style pizza were the first things I went in search of with a gang of my fellow junior officers upon our arrival in port. Like the futility of trying to drink just one of the very similar tall, red, fruity, potent and *expensive* "Hurricanes," at Pat O'Brian's off of Bourbon Street in New Orleans where that tropical drink was invented, having just one Subic Special took a self-discipline neither I nor any of my fellow junior officers possessed. Our youthful lack of good judgement at the time, combined with the easy access to good, cheap, fruity, and deceivingly strong drinks, reinforced the Subic Special experience.

Our in-port work days on the ship were busy, hot, and very demanding due to the arrival of a whole new army of shipyard workers and long lists of repairs and preservation activities for the ship's crew to accomplish each day before liberty call. For those not on the stay-on-board duty section, however, the off duty experience of Subic was one best described as surreal. It was, of course, great fun to sit in the western-themed Chuck Wagon eating pizza and getting smashed while a pretty young Filipino performer beautifully sang the overly-requested song "By the time I get to Penix" (requested only because wildly immature sailors knew she couldn't make the "f" sound in "Phoenix." But it was fun in a different way to get into civilian clothes each night, put your money and ID card in one of your shoes so they wouldn't be lost to the ubiquitous kid pickpockets, and head out to cross Shit River into the sweating, writhing, and deafening whirlpool of drunken debauchery that was Olongapo City.

Shit River was the aptly nicknamed waterway over which a narrow bridge was the only pathway from the base's gate to the main street of Olongapo. The waterway contained the drainage of much of the city's untreated sewage system on its way to the bay, and the smell conveyed as much. Day after day and night after night, there would always be at least a half dozen small boats below the bridge, each carrying a teen-aged girl standing up and dressed almost identically in white jeans and colorful shirt, both skin-tight, with a headband that matched the color of the shirt. The boats were paddled by the girls' brothers sitting in the stern. Each girl held a cone-shaped wire basket and called out to the sailors walking across the bridge to toss coins to them. The girls would do their best to catch the coins in their baskets, but there were always a few sailors who were mean-spirited and intentionally tossed coins just slightly out of reach of the girl so they would land in the water. Those coins would be quickly retrieved by another little brother who was in the sewage-strewn water, holding onto the side of the boat ready to dive down in the murk to find them. That this practice – and some of the practices that awaited us in the town – was not simply outlawed by either the city authorities or the U.S. Navy base commander was pretty pathetic. But that was what abjectly poor people had to do – send their kids onto and into Shit River. Deeply saddening.

The noise was the first thing that assaulted you in Olongapo, unless, of course, you'd not already been accosted either on or near the bridge by a pickpocket, or more likely a gang of them working together. Most of the din came from poorly muffled engine exhausts and constantly blown car horns, except there were very few cars. The vehicles found there for transportation, thousands of them, were *Jeepneys*. These were garishly painted and modified American Jeeps that had been abandoned decades ago by the tens of thousands at the end of WWII and turned into what was a uniquely Filipino mode of public transportation. The paint jobs were tremendously intricate with brightly colored designs, augmented by the imaginative application of stickers, lights, reflectors, flags, and the like. The structural modifications were in the form of extensions of the rear to create various configurations of seating, some able to accommodate a dozen riders or more. Instead of fixed taxi stop locations, people would hop on or hop off a Jeepney, sometimes while it was still moving, even though it was packed with riders. Payment was made by passing up to the driver a small denomination coin – certainly not a whole peso, the primary unit of currency. While many sailors used the Jeepneys to get as quickly as possible to their favorite bars, my fellow officers and I seldom rode them because doing so was a little more adventure than we were interested in. There were also a few "normal" taxis and we would generally hire one of them, even though this cost a little more.

The second sound you heard was the chorus of street-side vendors, almost always young boys, selling grilled meat on sticks. Each would try to entice you by waving the skewered meat and shouting "barbeque!" which always sounded like "BarBaCueoooooo!" No doubt because it had been marinated in soy sauce, garlic, and other spices, it always smelled delicious. But, not knowing what kind of meat it actually was kept many of us from indulging, at least before we'd attained a deep state of intoxication. The general assumption was that it could just as well have been dog or monkey as beef or chicken and, not trusting its safety, I personally never tried the stuff. But most sailors, especially the drunk ones, bought them like candy!

And the third dominant sound, which was not at all unpleasant, came from almost every one of the multitude of bars' open doors. Many of these grungy little bars in this dirt poor town had live music with very talented musicians and singers. You could literally choose your bar based on the kind of music they presented: rock 'n roll, country/western, jazz, Motown, etc., and you would hear near perfect imitations of popular groups like the Rolling Stones, Beatles, Supremes, etc. As a result, the entertainment was awesome.

Surprisingly, there were also a few legitimate places one could go to just for a meal. Our favorite was a Mexican restaurant a short cab ride from the bridge called Papa Gallo's, or some variant on that spelling. The food and margaritas were so good, relative to what else was available at other places we tried, that we ate there frequently, even with the full understanding that there was about a fifty-fifty chance we'd pay the price with diarrhea the next day. But that risk existed anywhere you might eat, and the price for a meal and a few drinks there was only five or six bucks. The going price of an ice cold San Miguel, a Filipino beer – the *only* beer you could find – was a single peso, about thirty five cents. And after dinner, we'd go in search of more San Miguel beers (or as we called them, "San Magoo's"), the easiest search on the planet.

I don't want to be too graphic in describing the lowest rung on the bar scene ladder, but it would be too glaring an omission not to acknowledge it. Simply put, if observing naked young women do things that might involve props such as cigarettes or coinage was what you were looking for, you could easily find places to do it. And sadly, there were enough sailors, other service members, and expats roaming the streets of Olongapo to keep several of those establishments open.

But the vast majority of the bars were places where drinks were cheap, music was good to great, and the girls were young and very pretty. As I said earlier, one had to make the decision whether to observe the spectacle of Olongapo or participate in it, and it was each girl's job to make sure there was minimum observation and maximum participation. That meant paying high drink prices at the bar for their company and then paying them somewhere else for their *company*. To me as a committed observer, the scene could be wildly entertaining, made further enjoyable by cold San Miguels at only a peso each. Because I wouldn't allow myself to slide down the slippery slope of participation, I had to develop my defense strategies. My approach, and generally that of most officers, was to blend in with the crowd at a table in a corner, drink a dozen pesos worth, and then stumble back to the ship intact (both physically and morally). But that meant fending off the young ladies who had the responsibility of making sure several hundred pesos, rather than a dozen, ended up in their hands, and, in turn, the pockets of their employers.

In every bar in Olongapo, and, in more or less all sailor bars all over the world, you would find an older woman who managed her young charges with a keen eye for profit. She was always called the MamaSan, and her position commanded no small amount of respect. Any customer who was not already buying drinks for a girl was quickly identified and targeted. The goal was to get this guy to start buying drinks for one of the young ladies. The over-priced fruit or wine drinks he would buy for her (generally five to ten pesos each) were lucrative, but this wasn't the most profitable element of the enterprise. It was the girl's job to turn the lap-sitting and expensive drink-sipping into a trip with her to a back room or upstairs, or to her own place for a short time or the entire night (referred to as "loving you long time"), depending on the price negotiated. Letting a guy like me just sit there drinking a few one peso beers was actually costing them money, and it wasn't good for business. And so avoiding being lured into the temptation of sex required a modicum of sobriety, an ironclad determination, and a strategy.

One could simply shoo off each girl that tried to sit on your lap or snuggle up to you. In spite of how that would seem to make good sense, it was actually a lousy strategy because the girls were relentless. Asking them to leave you alone would irritate them and, more importantly, irritate the MamaSan. Sooner or later, you'd very likely be asked to leave.

But since I enjoyed the spectacle of the Olongapo bars and I had a very clear "no fooling around" policy, there were a number of other strategies I tried at various times. One was saying to the girl who had placed herself on your lap, "Hey, I'm sorry, but I'm married." This never worked, though, because the predictable and instant reply was always something like, "Hey, Joe, *everybody's* married, Joe!" Or another approach, saying to the girl, "Hey, I'm sorry, but I'm a Catholic." The girl's (actually truthful) reply would be, "Me too, Joe. We can go to mass together tomorrow." Or there was a third strategy, saying to the girl, "Hey, I'm sorry, but I have a girlfriend in another bar." This option was not recommended, in spite of the fact that it might actually work. It could work because the one working girl on your lap would likely back off, showing professional courtesy to another working girl she didn't even know, since you might be that other girl's meal ticket, or even more importantly, you might be planning to rescue the other girl from this horrible life by bringing her to the States. Getting married to an American was truly like buying the winning lottery ticket for these ladies. But, as I said, using this strategy wasn't a good idea because if the management of the bar, or the girl you said it to, were to find out you were lying, you could maybe end up dead. Stories of sailors getting stabbed to death for playing games like this were talked about, and I guessed some of them were true.

In the end, the only tried and true strategy, option number four, was to go over to the MamaSan and give her something like twenty or so pesos and say, "Hey ma'am, the ladies here are very beautiful, but I'd like to be left alone. Is this enough?" After a quick negotiation and the payoff, you could go back to your seat, and be left alone, and everybody was happy. The bar had still made a little bit of money, and they knew you were going to stay and drink *there* for the rest of the night because they knew you wouldn't want to have to pay off the MamaSan in more than one bar. But the rule was that when you came back to that same bar the next night, the game would start all over again.

One night, however, during one of the several stops we were to make at Subic Bay over the next few months, something unusual and very special happened. Maybe because they liked the music, or they'd won over the MamaSan, or because it was friendly, or because the beer was extra cold… or for some other reason… some of the *Stoddert* officers had started to frequent one bar in particular, called the New Jolo Club. I had been there once or twice and didn't particularly care for it for two reasons I can remember. There was a small fenced-in pond out in front of it in which lived a small crocodile, and a nearby vendor sold small, live critters to sailors who would feed them to the beast just for the perverse fun of it. The "foods" being sold were intentionally chosen because they were cute, like ducklings. It was among the lowest of low brow entertainment, and I wasn't a fan. The second reason I didn't care for it was that the club was also known for having a back room where some of those aforementioned female performers astonished the clientele with skills no one should need to acquire. But, in many aspects, it was just another one of the many, many bars with girls, booze, and music for the sailors. And, as I said, some of our officers liked to go to the New Jolo Club.

So I was having dinner on board one evening, planning not to go out into town *again,* but knowing deep down I would. In walked one of our officers, who I can't remember, and he said we all needed to come with him right away and not to ask questions. We all asked, of course, where we were going. All he would say was, "New Jolo, but it's not what you think." And it wasn't.

Because of our colleague's enthusiasm and persuasiveness, and because the offer of an adventure was attractive, we agreed and quickly got into our civvies, stuffed our money and ID's into our shoes as always, and left the ship to "jump the ditch," our shorthand for crossing Shit River and going into Olongapo. There were about eight of us in the group, just the right number to commandeer a Jeepney, and we soon arrived at the New Jolo Club. We were surprised to be greeted at the door by the manager (I had yet to actually meet the male manager of *any* Olongapo bar!), and he introduced himself as Rick. He was a large man for a Filipino, and from his appearance, you probably wouldn't want to cross him. Toughness was likely one of the most important prerequisites for the job of Olongapo bar manager. But Rick was smiling and friendly, which made us all suspicious, except for the shipmate who had brought us. He and Rick knew each other. How this was so we never did learn, but it was probably best not to ask.

Rick took us to a back room and offered us each a cold beer for free. Free was not something that happened very often in that town. Each of us was presented with the gift of a brand new long-sleeved white shirt, folded and wrapped in cellophane. Some were beautifully embroidered cotton and some, including mine, were made of a dense lace. We were told they were Barong Tagalog formal shirts, lightweight and worn loose, not tucked into the trousers. I learned they're traditionally worn by gentlemen at weddings and special occasions – essentially Filipino tuxedoes. We took off our shirts and put on these very nice new shirts, becoming yet more curious about what was going on.

Rick then explained that this was a very special evening at the New Jolo Club. The club was closed for the night because this was *their* night to do something special for themselves, as they did each year at this time. We were to be honored guests and the formal on-stage escorts for the ladies competing for the title of *Miss New Jolo!* We looked at each other in astonishment, and a little relief that no one was getting married. We soon realized we were the only non-locals in the place, a rare and fascinating opportunity to participate in the culture in a way that was more meaningful and noble to them than selling beer and sex to drunk sailors – actually honoring their daughters and sisters for their beauty and substance. What ensued was a no-kidding beauty pageant patterned after the international Miss Universe contest, complete with evening gowns, swimsuits, and interview rounds. There was nothing phony about it, and each young lady truly hoped to win the crown.

Formally attired and instructed about our responsibilities, we were introduced to the contestant we would soon escort onto the stage in the opening ceremony. Each young lady was beautifully dressed in an elegant evening gown. Many wore flowers in intricately upswept hair styles, and each wore a sash with the name of a Filipino city such as Miss Manila, etc. Surprisingly, there was no Miss Olongapo. I don't know if this was to hide the fact that these were the same bar girls and strippers you could see there every night, and using the cities they came from, or wished they did, was more dignified than confirming where they worked their trade. But on that evening, they were ladies.

While still backstage, we were introduced to the master of ceremonies, a similarly dressed, good looking middle-aged man, who wrote down each of our names and ranks. When all was ready, the host emerged through the curtains onto the small, theatrically-lit stage and welcomed the well-dressed audience (again, all Filipino) that packed the club. And then, while a live band played tasteful music, he introduced each young lady taking the stage on the arm of one of us officers, also saying the name and rank of each lady's escort. With all contestants and escorts on the stage, the host sang to them in his best Bert Parks imitation. It was all done in English, which was surprising, but perhaps this was again in imitation of the international beauty pageants they had seen on TV, which were always in English.

After these introductions and the song, the entourage left the stage, and we men were shown to seats in a prominent location in the front. The host thanked the officers of the *USS Benjamin Stoddert* for acting as escorts, and for the rest of the evening, we were treated as honored guests, and were never once asked to pay for any food or drinks. Nor did we take undue advantage of the generous hospitality and treatment being shown to us as their honored guests, meaning none of us drank enough to be intoxicated. For one evening, we knew these young women weren't being exploited for our amusement, and we were not going to spoil their night or do anything "unbecoming of an officer and a gentleman." All other nights, Rick was no doubt a ruthless bouncer and exploiter of the young women. But for that one night, though, they were Misses Universe with Bert Parks making them feel like a million bucks and a million miles away from their sad circumstances. It was a magical transformation that I wished could last for more than one night for them.

Looking back on that evening, I feel truly honored that my fellow officers and I were given a chance to see through the pragmatic nature of an impoverished people surviving in Olongapo by doing what they needed to do in the booze and sex trade. The dollars spent by American sailors and contractors meant that their families would survive. Nevertheless, the Filipino culture of refinement, respect, and dignity prevailed, at lease for one night.

As the situation in Vietnam continued to grow ever increasingly grim at the start of 1975, and as we looked forward to several more months of our WestPac deployment, I began to develop a whole new attitude toward the Philippines and its people as a result of that evening. Subic and Olongapo would be our base of operation for the rest of the cruise, and I would spend more evenings on liberty in town, and I even returned there on our ship's next deployment a year and a half later. But the bars had lost most of their attraction for me. I was still a fascinated observer of the scene and, of course, I still enjoyed the music and cold beer. But I never went back to that particular night club because I couldn't bear to see the newly crowned and very beautiful Miss New Jolo, or her fellow contestants, working their sad circumstances-driven profession. My memory of that evening would forever make Subic special.

CHAPTER 10

An Indian Ocean and African Adventure

WASHINGTON – The U.S. task force headed by the nuclear-powered aircraft carrier Enterprise with 80 planes aboard will be the sixth American carrier force to enter the Indian Ocean since the October 1973 Middle East war led to a generally higher U.S. Naval presence in the area. It will also mark the Indian Ocean debut of the U.S. Navy's new F-14 jet fighters which are usually deployed in high threat areas. The six ship Enterprise group left Subic Bay on Tuesday and was expected to pass through the Malacca Straits into the Indian Ocean over the weekend, although the task force destination has never been officially announced... The Soviets plan to send more of their Vladivostok-based Pacific fleet units through the South China Sea to warm waters in the Indian Ocean during the winter months when their home ports are frozen over, according to intelligence reports... The non-governmental Center for Defense Information says the Enterprise is accompanied by the nuclear guided missile cruiser Long Beach, the guided missile destroyer Stoddert, a destroyer escort, and two oilers.

USS ENTERPRISE CVAN 65 LEDGER (shipboard newsletter), January 13, 1975

The *Enterprise*, with her sophisticated communications capabilities, was able to access a national news wire report to inform their crew, through their daily onboard newsletter, what was going on in the world.

I have no doubt this was particularly interesting when their own ship was mentioned in the news. Most of the thousands of sailors on an aircraft carrier usually have no idea where they are at any given time unless the briefer from the ship's Meteorological Office shows them where they are on weather charts used for the nightly weather briefing televised throughout the ship. But over on the *Benjamin Stoddert,* our captain regularly updated us with our whereabouts over the ship's 1MC public address system. It was never surprising but good to know nonetheless.

But life in the Navy has a way of surprising you when you least expect it, like finding out one morning we were about to sail into the Indian Ocean and observe weather conditions I had studied for my graduate thesis just a year earlier. Suddenly, I felt like I was a big fish in a smallish pond.

The Chagos Archipelago is a small, isolated island group in the middle of the Indian Ocean, about 950 nautical miles south of the tip of India. The largest of the islands is Diego Garcia, which today is home to a U.S. logistics base which has been of tremendous strategic importance to American naval and air operations in that theater through the various crises in Southwest Asia over the past couple of decades. But in the 1970s, it was just a nearly-deserted, sleepy, just-above-sea-level coral island surrounding a peaceful blue lagoon. Sometime in 1971, the British, who had long maintained a presence there, began to launch weather balloons with radiosonde sensors from the island to measure the temperature and humidity structure of the upper atmosphere there. With the commencement of these twice daily upper air "soundings," openly available to the world through the United Nation's World Meteorological Organization, the international weather community gained a tremendously important new source of data to feed global atmospheric computer models. This "numerical modeling" was, at that time, in its infancy, but nevertheless, it was a stunning revolution in weather forecasting. Today, we take for granted the accuracy of extremely sophisticated computer models running in powerful supercomputers. These computing centers are in the United States (the NOAA Center for Environment and Climate Prediction in College Park, Maryland and the Navy's Fleet Numerical Meteorology and Oceanography Center in Monterey, California), in Great Britain (the European Centre for Medium-Range Weather Forecasting in Reading, UK), and a few other locations. Their atmospheric models are fed not just by data from weather balloons and surface observations, but also by huge amounts of weather and ocean data collected by satellites.

The collection of upper air data from the middle of the Indian Ocean in the early 1970s was an extremely important new source of observations for the fledgling numerical weather models, and also for the atmospheric science research community, particularly for those who specialized in tropical meteorology. For the first time, they could use those observations from Diego Garcia with other observations made at stations in Indonesia, India, and eastern Africa to try to better understand the generation mechanisms and three dimensional structure of tropical storms in that ocean basin. Tropical cyclones in the Indian Ocean, like hurricanes in the Atlantic and typhoons in the western Pacific, begin as north-south undulations of the easterly trade winds near the equator. Those undulations, or tropical waves, are fed by energy from the warm ocean surface and grow in amplitude until they spin off into a counter-clockwise rotation around a low atmospheric pressure center – giving birth to tropical storms. These mechanisms were already well understood by the research community for the Atlantic and Pacific, but because there had been no data source in the middle of the Indian Ocean, the new Diego Garcia upper air observations presented a tremendous opportunity to better understand tropical meteorology in that vast ocean.

Few would get the opportunity to begin the exploitation of those observations at a research university focusing on tropical meteorology. Fewer still would get to do so at the prestigious U.S. Naval Postgraduate School (NPS) in Monterey, California which provides Master's and Doctoral degrees to mid-grade Navy officers, and a small number of officers from the other services or from allied nations. It doesn't enroll civilians except a few government employees. And very few of the servicemen who get selected to attend are freshly minted Ensigns from the Naval Academy selected for the Immediate Graduation Education Program (IGEP). I was one of those lucky few.

In July, 1973, fresh from graduating from the Naval Academy and getting married, I found myself extremely fortunate to be enrolled in the one-year IGEP at NPS with an opportunity to earn my master's degree in meteorology.

So there I was, one of a handful of Ensigns among the student body, which was almost entirely made up of officers two or three ranks senior to me. Most of them had already completed one or two tours of duty as surface ship drivers, submariners, aviators, or "boots on the ground" Marines in Vietnam. Those "normal" students were enrolled in a standard two and a half year program that gave them enough time to get back into an academic mode and rewarded them with the well-earned luxury of stability with their families in the beautiful surroundings of Monterey Bay and Carmel. However, mine was an intensive one year program heavily loaded with classes in addition to research, and the huge task of writing a thesis. My academic advisor was Dr. George Haltiner, a world renowned pioneer in the field of numerical (computer) weather prediction and chair of the meteorology department, who would later become a dear friend. Shortly after I had arrived at NPS, he asked me to come to his office and, upon entering, I was warmly greeted with, "Ensign Malay, we have a thesis for you!"

With that, he introduced me to my advisor, Dr. Chei Pei Chang (who went by C.P.), who was already my professor for a tropical meteorology course.

On a large table in the office sat several neat piles of paper which, if stacked together, would have been about ten feet tall. George pointed to the piles and said, "*This* is your thesis!" The two professors explained that what they had obtained – and which to their knowledge existed nowhere else on earth – were the photocopied observations of all radiosonde balloon sounding (upper air measurements of temperature, moisture, wind direction, and speed vs. altitude) and surface pressure, temperature, and humidity observations from *all* Indian Ocean basin stations from the time observations had begun on Diego Garcia two years before. They had pulled many strings to obtain all this data and then realized they had underestimated what it would take to process and analyze it. So they handed it all to me to "do something with" under the guidance of C.P. Chang. The only words I could muster, from my best Naval Academy training, were, "Aye aye, sirs!"

"Spectrum Analysis of Tropical Waves in the Indian Ocean" was the title of my successfully written and defended thesis about nine months later. It was completed only after all of those observations were hand-written onto IBM punch card coding sheets by breaking the meteorological code they were in down to the various elements of temperature, pressure, wind, etc. It was a massive task that took myself and a weather technician on the staff two or three weeks to accomplish. Then, each line of the coding sheets had to be typed by two key punch operators to create about twenty eighteen inch deep boxes of IBM data card decks. Then the thousands of cards had to be run through a special computer program on the school's IBM 360 mainframe computer system. The meteorological technician who was assigned to help me do the coding sheets and the two lady key punch operators are probably still having nightmares about that experience today. I think George and C.P. would have passed me on my master's just for the massive effort required to manage that ten foot high stack of data sheets. But as a result of what were, at that time, groundbreaking discoveries of statistically significant correlations among various parameters across the Indian Ocean basin, I became somewhat of an expert on the mechanisms and structures of tropical storms in that ocean. When I received my diploma and orders to report to the *US Benjamin Stoddert,* I figured it would almost certainly be the last time I would ever think about tropical weather in the Indian Ocean.

And so, there I was in January, 1975, about to embark on a voyage through the Strait of Malacca and out onto that wide open and *almost* unknown expanse. There was, at that time, no Somali or Yemeni piracy (at least that the United States knew or cared about), and no American base on Diego Garcia. Other than the island-based observations I had used for my research and widely scattered observations from the continents and islands on the fringe of the ocean, which amounted to a small fraction of the data we collect out there today, there was almost no meteorological, oceanographic, or hydrographic (bathymetric survey) data for the vast Indian Ocean from Indonesia to the Indian subcontinent and to the coast of Africa and the entrance to the Persian Gulf or Red Sea. U.S. Navy ships would very rarely visit the area, but there we were, assigned to serve as an escort for the *Enterprise* as part of a small task force entering the Indian Ocean on a "show the flag" mission to establish American presence there. The Soviet Union was routinely sending its ships there, and ours was just the beginning of more frequent visits by the U.S. Navy.

The Strait of Malacca separates the Malay Peninsula to the north and Indonesia to the south, and the channel is critical for commercial shipping. At its narrowest point, it's only about one and a half nautical miles across, which is wide enough to allow for the heavy ship traffic to proceed safely. Most of the time.

While were eating lunch during our passage through the strait, with the captain, executive officer, and those officers not on watch at the wardroom table, the phone mounted to the table leg by the CO's left knee rang. He picked it up, listened for a few seconds… said "OK" … and left the table quickly without saying anything to the rest of us. He had seemed calm, and such calls with requests for the commanding officer to come to the bridge were common, so we continued eating and chatting normally. About five minutes later, the ship abruptly lurched as if hitting a big wave then settled back down. A few minutes later, the captain came back, took his seat, and resumed eating, again without saying anything. We later learned that we had missed colliding with a merchant vessel by a matter of feet. After calmly leaving the lunch table, Captain Siegrist had climbed the stairs to the bridge, assessed the situation quickly, and issued the exact and correct orders for course and speed necessary to avoid the collision. And then he returned to his lunch as though it was just another day at the office. That was seamanship.

Even though my job on the *Stoddert* really had nothing to do with meteorology, Captain Siegrist often made it clear he liked having "a weather guesser" in his wardroom. During any appearance of heavy weather or unexpected changes to the weather, I was asked to interpret the sometimes cryptic forecasts we received from the Fleet Weather Central office in Guam.

Once, when I was working somewhere in the bowels of the ship, I heard over the 1MC ship-wide loudspeaker system, "Ensign Malay to the bridge! Ensign Malay to the bridge!" Generally, when an officer is called *by name* to the bridge, it's not a good thing. The one person who was allowed to use the 1MC for that purpose was the captain. So I remember hauling ass up to the bridge and arriving out of breath, having climbed several ladders to get there. (Steep stairways on a ship are referred to in nautical language as ladders.) As I entered the bridge anticipating certain doom, I blurted out the obligatory, "Request permission to enter the bridge, sir," to the officer of the deck and, without waiting for the pro forma reply, "granted," I saw Captain Siegrist waving to me from one of the bridge wings with a look of excitement on his face.

"Quick! Get out here," he said. Startled, I hustled over to him and he put an arm around my shoulder and pointed toward the sky with his other arm.

"See that, Jon? Do you know what that is? That's the back of the front!" And he howled with laughter. What he pointed to was a line of clouds. It had occurred to him that he could have some fun with his "weather guy." I got the joke and, with a huge sense of relief, laughed right along with him. But *nobody* enjoyed that joke as much as Ed Siegrist did!

About fifteen years later, Sharon and I attended a cocktail party at the home of my shipmate and classmate, Jim Moseman, and his wife Emily. (You may recall that Jim was the "perp" of the famous theft of executive officer Pete Finch's stateroom door.) To my surprise, I was introduced by the Mosemans to a young woman who was Captain Siegrist's adult daughter. About five minutes into our conversation, in which I talked about how much I enjoyed working for her dad, she stopped me and said, "Oh my God, you're the back of the front guy, aren't you?" Over the years, Ed had talked about the joke he had played on his junior officer with his family and probably many other people. Now flash forward another twenty years and, while attending my first reunion of the *USS Benjamin Stoddert Association* in northern California, I very happily ran into Ed and his wife, Evie. And the first words he said after we exclaimed our excitement and joy at seeing each other were, "Evie, this is Jon Malay. Remember him? He's the back of the front guy!"

Returning to my story with the ship in Subic Bay prior to getting underway for the Indian Ocean, but not leaving the subject of weather, an opportunity for me to use my meteorology and oceanography experience came up. Before leaving port, we were visited by an officer from the *Enterprise,* and I was summoned to the meeting. Arriving in the wardroom, I found the captain, the XO, and the meteorological officer from the aircraft carrier, Lieutenant Commander Dick Stender. He said he'd heard that *Stoddert* had a meteorologist on board and so he had a special request for me. He hoped I would be willing to take personal oversight of the careful logging of all of *Stoddert's* weather and seawater temperature observations – a responsibility normally borne on a destroyer by the ship's navigator and antisubmarine warfare officer – and also carefully record my own personal observations and that of the crew of any additional atmospheric or oceanographic phenomenon that might be observed while we were in the Indian Ocean. He explained something I already knew: that there was a severe dearth of observational data about that ocean and that it was likely that American military operations would become more frequent in that theater. Every piece of information about the environment would help fill in the blanks.

In enthusiastically agreeing to do all of this, I explained to him the circumstances of my master's thesis on Indian Ocean weather, and he was delighted to have the right guy for the job. And he said I was the right guy for another job as well, while he was at it. He handed me a wooden disk that looked to be about one foot in diameter, which had apparently been cut from a hardwood board by the *Enterprise's* wood shop.

"Know what this is?" he asked.

"Well, I'm guessing you want me to turn it into a Secchi Disk, right, sir?" He smiled and confirmed my guess. Secchi Disks are oceanographic measurement tools that are painted white and always the same in diameter of thirty centimeters or twelve inches. The disk is weighted and lowered into the water by a rope attached to its center until it just barely becomes un-seeable, and then pulled up until the observer can just barely see it. That "optical depth" is determined by measuring the rope's length from the disk to the waterline. Even though there's an element of subjectivity because of different observers' visual acuity and varying degrees of cloud cover, this process still yields a primitive but reasonably accurate measurement of the ocean's clarity, or more precisely its converse, the turbidity. Commander Stender's request meant my Bos'n Mates would need to paint the disk and rig it with weights and a measuring line (with knots at one foot intervals) and then the ship would have to stop dead in the water once a day at local apparent noon (the moment of maximum overhead sun angle, as measured by the navigator using a sextant), so that I could make my observations. Of course, Captain Siegrist and I happily agreed we would do our best.

I've always looked forward to the lunch hour, but in the middle of the Indian Ocean, I came to dread the strike of noon. Stopping a 437 foot long destroyer *exactly* dead in the water is no small feat. Wood chips are thrown overboard so the officers on the bridge could determine when the ship was completely stopped. We did this every day for several days, even though trying to maintain a screening position on a nuclear aircraft carrier that would just continue along and then demand that we catch up. My daily Secchi Disk observations – even though expected by the captain – made me a very unpopular guy with the bridge watch-standers. But not for much longer.

On one particular day when we were halfway across the ocean, the low-lying topography of the island of Diego Garcia became just barely visible in the distance. The ship had once again stopped at noon for my observation, which I would do from the middle of the port side main deck for consistency. I began to lower the white disk into the very clear and deep blue tropical water. I was guessing it would be a deeper measurement than usual due to the unusually calm sea and what seemed to be a low amount of microscopic biological stuff (which oceanographers call "critters.") Lower and lower the disk went, until the rope went slack with the just barely visible disk sitting on the bottom!

I immediately knew this was a bad thing. Encounters by a ship's hull with the sea bottom were never good and usually very bad for the careers of captains, navigators, and officers of the deck. But I didn't have time to contemplate any of that because, while the disk was still down there on the sea floor, the ship started to move. The disk was being dragged and had therefore become a "sea anchor." With my arm strength alone I couldn't retrieve it, so I wrapped a few turns of the line – a half inch diameter nylon fiber rope – around a railing stanchion and held it tight. I watched in horror as the line tautened very quickly. Nylon line stretches quite a bit before breaking, and I began to fear the line would part, creating a potentially man-killing recoil of the severed end. Since I would be the man getting killed, I quickly let the onboard end of the rope slip through my hands and the disk and the line disappeared astern as we picked up speed.

I was confused by what had happened and more than a little pissed off, so I huffed up to the bridge where I found an unnatural silence and strained looks on the faces of the officers standing watch. While I had been prepared to blurt out "what the f---?" I went instead to the officer of the deck, my friend and mentor Pete Coste, and quietly asked what was happening. It's a good thing I asked calmly because he gave me a dark look that told me it was *he* who was thoroughly pissed off.

It turns out the *Enterprise,* several miles away, had called us on the radio in unencrypted plain voice – normally used only in emergencies – and said something like, "*Stoddert,* we have indications your position is in very shallow water. Request advise." In Navy terminology, "Request advise" means, "Immediately report what's going on over there!" There had been a rush to the navigator's table to look at the chart on which our position would be marked, and to everyone's horror, the ship's position and recent track had *not* been plotted on a navigational chart – a chart with land masses, depths, and known shoal locations marked. The quartermaster of the watch, not being able to find the appropriate chart for that location, had switched to a celestial navigation plotting sheet – a special kind of chart with all of the latitude/longitude markings of a normal chart used in plotting star/planet observations, but not having any surface or subsurface features printed on it. This was, of course, unthinkable, embarrassing, and dangerous. And so a navigation chart was hastily found and our last known position was plotted. It showed we had indeed sailed into a shallow area in the Chagos Rise. Fortunately, we were soon in deep water out of harm's way, without having touched bottom. It's probably a good thing we had a reason to stop at noon that day.

At the captain's insistence, neither our Secchi Disk measurements nor that incident were ever mentioned again. And there were, of course, no more measurements from that time forward. At the end of our Indian Ocean trip, I submitted everything I had recorded by mail to Lieutenant Commander Stender on the *Enterprise,* but never received any thanks or acknowledgement from him. There we no questions about why the Secchi observations ended abruptly halfway across to Africa. And having myself served as an aircraft carrier meteorological officer exactly ten years later, I now know how busy life can be trying to keep two senior captains (the carrier's commanding officer and the air wing commander) plus one Rear Admiral (the battle group commander) all happy. If the weather was bad, all three of those guys were really unhappy, and there was never a damn thing I could do about it when they seemed to imply it was all my fault. Weather officers can only share their frustrations with God, because we know He's in production and the weather office is just in sales. It was disappointing that my Indian Ocean observations hadn't been acknowledged in any way, but I was much happier we'd not run aground.

Being seasoned mariners, the captain and about half of the crew were members of the "Ancient Order of the Deep" known as Shellbacks. That esteemed title meant that at some earlier point in their seagoing careers, they had begun a day as "Scurvy Polywogs," and, as the ship crossed the Equator, they were appropriately indoctrinated and welcomed into the order of Shellbacks in an age old ceremony called "Crossing the Line." With our destination of Mombasa, Kenya lying at four degrees south latitude, it was inevitable that we'd experience a line crossing – and *experience* is the only way to describe the day-long event. I won't divulge in these pages the secrets of this ancient ceremony as practiced by modern U.S. Navy ships, other than to say it was, for us lowly "Wogs," degrading, challenging, smelly, a little painful, and outrageously fun. That today I count myself among the loyal subjects of King Neptune and his royal scribe Davey Jones as a Trusty Shellback comes with no small amount of pride. I still have my Shellback certificate, embossed with the ship's seal and signed by the commanding officer, which proves I'm a Shellback and will *never* have to go through another indoctrination. There was no crossing the line ceremony on our return trip from Mombasa because the entire crew was made up of Trusty Shellbacks. Unfortunately, though, I never again crossed the equator on a ship so I've never been on the other side of a Shellback ceremony. Maybe someday…

Late on the very dark, moonless night before we entered the port of Mombasa, I was up on deck looking at the stars, as were several of us who were too excited to sleep. The *Enterprise* was invisible, out there somewhere over the horizon, but in what direction I wasn't sure. Behind us to the east a strange glow slowly appeared on the horizon. We more or less assumed it was the *Enterprise* illuminating all of her flight deck and superstructure lights. That wasn't completely unheard of for aircraft carriers, even though it violated the "rules of the nautical road" for nighttime navigational lights. But we'd never seen lights as bright as this on her in the two weeks of sailing together. As the glow on the horizon grew steadily brighter, the mystery deepened. I stepped onto the bridge and asked the officers on watch if they knew what it was, and they were equally mystified except to say they were tracking a very large ship on radar, and it wasn't the *Enterprise*, which was over the horizon in another direction entirely. Eventually, in all of her blazing glory, the Cunard Line's *Queen Elizabeth II* sailed within our direct view, heading toward a port visit at Mombasa just as we were. One might suspect that her transit across the Indian Ocean had been more fun than ours, and if they had held a Crossing-the-Line ceremony, it included champagne served in crystal flutes. But if I ever cross the Equator on a cruise ship, I'll still be sure to have my Shellback certificate with me to make sure I receive the respect due to a member of that distinguished and ancient order.

On entering port the next morning, I had the opportunity to witness some of the most complex and dangerous ship-handling I ever experienced in my naval career, and my already huge respect for my captain grew yet greater. While the *Enterprise* anchored way out in deep water and sent her liberty parties ashore in hired ferries, *Stoddert* sailed up a narrow river to a confluence of two streams where the captain had just enough room to maneuver the ship in a 180 degree turn without asking for any help from either of the two tugboats standing by. We moored between buoys fore and aft near the side of the channel, just yards from an unforgiving shore – and all this while the wind whistled and pushed us in directions we didn't want to go. I was in awe of how he did it, and in awe of how the Bos'n Mates working for me got us tied to those buoys when I was convinced somebody was going to get killed and/or we would run aground. I thank God neither of those things happened.

Our visit to Mombasa was intended to serve as a new extension of American naval power into a geographic region that had been ignored during our decades of concentrating that power almost exclusively in Southeast Asia. But it was also an opportunity for us American sailors to experience a new culture while also enjoying several days of great liberty ashore. For me, seeing commercial ships at the docks with "Zanzibar" on their sterns under their ships' names; taking a safari to the Tsavo National Park replete with elephants, lions, and every sort of African big game one would hope to see; drinking Tusker Lager in a bar while watching men slaughter a goat across the street; enjoying an elegant dinner at the British club… these are among my favorite African memories. But seeing a Kentucky Fried Chicken restaurant in 1975 on the hot and dusty main street of Mombasa was probably the most surprising of all the things we saw. My fellow officers and I did NOT dine with the Colonel.

After our delightful visit to Kenya, we were again at sea, but this time without the *Enterprise*. On February 6, the island of Mauritius, which lies just under 1,500 nautical miles southeast of Mombasa and 475 nautical miles east of Madagascar, suffered a direct hit by Tropical Cyclone Gervaise. It devastated the island, taking six lives and leaving nearly 4,000 people homeless. *Enterprise* and her crew were dispatched to render assistance in restoring power, water, and telephone service there.

Maybe it was because of the deteriorating situation in Vietnam, or maybe it was because the nuclear aircraft carrier could sprint at high speed to Mauritius without needing to refuel, but *Stoddert* wasn't sent with her. We made an uneventful transit back across the vast ocean, through the Strait and arrived in Singapore for a port visit on February 19, exactly 40 days since we had passed that city state on our way to Africa.

Singapore was quite simply a modern, affluent, clean, and fun port of call. I happily recall playing a softball game at their beautiful park called the Padang, a game in which the *Stoddert* crew was thoroughly crushed by a local club team who then treated us to ice cold beer. This was *déjà vu* of our earlier drubbing at tennis by the South Koreans, but it was fun. I also enjoyed playing squash, my favorite racquet game, particularly as we were introduced to a "British style" squash ball, which was much softer and slower than the balls we had used learning the game at the Naval Academy. We did our best to behave like proper gentlemen, drinking martinis, gin and tonics, or Pimm's Cups at the British military outpost, which was named, in characteristic British understatement, "Terror Barracks." And no visit to Singapore would have been complete without sipping sweet, cold, refreshing Singapore Slings at the famous Raffles Hotel. It was a relaxing six day visit. And having my last name Malay was the source of great fun when talking to the locals who lived in a city surrounded by Malaysia.

CHAPTER 11

Tedium Denied

WASHINGTON (AP) – Thailand's ambassador to Washington says a failure by Congress to vote emergency aid to Cambodia and South Vietnam would "be read in Asia as a sign the United States is abandoning its friends."
The Pioneer, Bemidji, Minnesota, Thursday, February 27, 1975

After leaving the Indian Ocean and enjoying what almost resembled vacations in Mombasa and Singapore, our attention turned to the bleak news coming out of South Vietnam. The North Vietnamese Army had begun an offensive aimed at finally conquering the south and was advancing quickly southward; the South Vietnamese government was falling apart. In spite of increasingly desperate attempts by President Ford to bolster our beleaguered ally by imploring Congress to appropriate and authorize funds for additional material support (but not American combat troops again), my shipmates and I began to realize the end was near, and the unavoidable outcome would be the defeat of the American-backed government in Saigon. We began to wonder what role, if any, the Seventh Fleet would play. At this point, nobody in our chain of command really knew. Clearly, there were contingencies being discussed at high levels, as one would expect of any well-run military force. I hoped the *Stoddert* crew wouldn't experience the tedium of spending the next couple of months of hot days in the sun, maintaining the ship, and many more nights of liberty in the circus of Olongapo. But I also feared worse things could happen. We just didn't know.

We didn't actually have much time to be bored, however. As soon as we tied up in Subic, the entire crew was put to work cleaning up the ship, giving her another new coat of paint from bow to stern, the relentless rust having finally popped through our beautiful Kaohsiung paint job, and getting our divisions' paperwork in order. We only had a week to prepare for a change of command. And for me, personally, it turned out to be an extraordinarily busy week.

Since I'd attended antisubmarine warfare officer and nuclear weapons handling officer schools in San Diego during the summer before reporting for duty on *Stoddert,* it was long planned that I would take over the ASW division from Lieutenant (Junior Grade) Dave Rau when he left the ship upon our return to Pearl Harbor. To prepare for that transition, I was no longer in charge of first (deck) division, which I turned over to my fellow Ensign Roger Wilson, who had just left his previous job in engineering. These changes were elements of a rotation of junior officer assignments to broaden their professional experiences. Roger, you may recall, was my betel nut buddy back in Kaohsiung, but he was now the First Lieutenant and my new roommate on board. I needed a new job for only the few months until we returned home, and, as I'd heard before, the XO called me to his stateroom/office and said, "Have we got a deal for you!" I was named overhaul manager (OM), to oversee the administrative preparations that had to be made before we arrived back at Pearl and went into the Shipyard for a year of repairs and renovations. There, in dry-dock, one of the more senior department heads, Lieutenant Eric Utegaard, our operations officer, would officially become the OM, and I would become shipyard liaison as his and the captain's right hand man.

When we'd arrived in Subic, I was given oversight of a team of visiting engineers from the Pearl Harbor Naval Shipyard who would, with the support of the Subic Bay Naval Shipyard, conduct what was known as the "Pre-Overhaul Test and Inspection (abbreviated POT&I and appropriately pronounced *pot and eye*). This was a huge challenge for me because I wasn't an engineer and the new CO was known to be among the best nuclear engineers in the Navy. I had no choice but to step up and give it my very best.

Every piece of gear on the ship, every compartment, every deck, and every system had to be visually inspected, discrepancies written down, and forms filled out. It was my job to explain to all of my fellow division officers and their department heads what was required, then harass them to do it, and then review all the results with the civilians from the shipyard and the ship's senior officers. Those results would be used to generate a long, long list of things the shipyard workers and our own ship's force would accomplish in our year-long overhaul. Captain Siegrist wanted very little to do with it, since he was about to turn over command. But I found an ally in our meticulous and truly brilliant XO, Pete Finch. More than once I had to invoke the threat of ratting out my fellow officers to the XO to get their cooperation. It all went just fine and, in Captain Siegrist's fitness report on me, my first since reporting aboard, he made it clear that he, the XO, and Rick Buttina, my department head, all thought I was doing very good work. There's nothing like a little praise to motivate an overworked sailor.

CHAPTER 12

Change of Command

PHNOM PENH, Cambodia (AP) – Heavy rebel gunfire and deadly mines on Friday halted a 2,000 man government drive aimed at pushing the insurgents out of the "rocket belt" around Phnom Penh airport, field reports said.

Forty miles southeast of Phnom Penh, government forces abandoned Sierra Two, their last outpost on the lower Mekong River. Military sources said the 800-man force was evacuated to the naval base town of Neak Luong, further lessoning any hopes of reopening the Mekong to resupply convoys soon....

In South Vietnam, thousands of government reinforcements backed by armored vehicles forces fought stiff battles with thousands of North Vietnamese troops in an effort to reopen a key highway in the central highlands, field reports said. The Saigon government charged that North Vietnam is cutting vital roads in the highlands for a large scale offensive.

Independent Press-Telegram, Long Beach, California,
Saturday, March 8, 1975

On March 8, 1975, it was time for us to say goodbye to our commanding officer, Ed Siegrist, who had reached the end of his tour of duty and was ready to take his next assignment at the well-deserved rank of Captain back home in the States.

Ed had truly become a father figure to me, and, no doubt, to my fellow junior officers and many of the crew. So even though a change of command is always a day of great celebration for the departing commander, receiving thanks and best wishes from his crew, it was also sad for all of us. This was particularly true with the quickly growing uncertainty of the situation in Vietnam and our possible role in the coming weeks.

Ed Siegrist's departure was quickly offset by the arrival of our new CO, Commander Peter M. Hekman, Jr., another truly outstanding leader. Pete was a nuclear power-trained officer who had been the Chief Engineer on the *Enterprise.* He'd been hand-chosen by the Commander of Naval Surface Forces, Pacific Fleet, to take our ship, desperately in need of major repairs and upgrades, through the year-long overhaul at the Pearl Harbor Naval Shipyard. Looking back at that overhaul experience, I can say without reservation that there could not possibly have been a better leader or more talented engineer who could make both the huge number of shipyard workers and the ship's crew perform for him with the smooth teamwork of a symphony orchestra – without the music or the clean clothes, no less!

Captain Hekman set about making many changes from day one, addressing things we had previously ignored or trivialized. This began with a thorough cleanup of the interior of the ship, which meant the overnight removal of the thousands of nudie pictures which had been taped to the bulkheads (walls) of virtually every berthing compartment and work space. Most of them had been there from the early years of the ship's Vietnam gun line duty and had simply been taken for granted as a kind of ubiquitous "wallpaper" all over the ship, even though it constituted a huge fire hazard. Their removal began immediately after Captain Hekman's first tour of the ship, and we were all amazed to find pristine gray paint beneath them, if a little sticky from years-old strips of yellowing tape. Surprisingly, there were zero complaints from the crew.

And happily for me, our new CO challenged the Chief Petty Officers' mess to either work with him or request to be put ashore for transfer, which quickly resulted in the surprising disappearance from the ship of my troublesome Chief Bos'n Mate Spicer. *Hallelujah!* I quickly found in Captain Hekman an extremely impressive and experienced officer from whom I would learn my craft as an officer like never before – or ever since. To have two back-to-back commanding officers with the skill, integrity, and positive and empowering leadership of Ed Siegrist and Pete Hekman made the officers and enlisted men of *Benjamin Stoddert* very fortunate indeed.

To this point, Captain Hekman had a favorite expression: "If you can't get your work done in twenty-four hours, you need to work nights." We junior officers secretly scratched our heads at this strange wording, but its meaning was crystal clear: work hard and don't quit until you get it done and done right. Captain Hekman worked harder than any of us, and he always got it right.

As luck would have it, we soon received the news that we would make a port call at Hong Kong, which had long been a highly prized treat for Navy ships deployed to WestPac. There had been talk of such a visit for weeks, but every positive-sounding rumor was checked by the pessimism that came with speculations about whatever was going to happen in Vietnam. The news from there was nothing but bad, and we were sure there would be no more "R&R" port calls, particularly at Hong Kong. That pessimism persisted right up to the moment we tied up to a mooring buoy in that spectacular harbor between the cities of Hong Kong and Kowloon, and the most welcome words in the Navy… "Now Liberty Call" … were announced over the 1MC speakers throughout the ship.

CHAPTER 13

The Easter Miracle

DA NANG, South Vietnam (UPI) – The last government troops surrendered the city of Hue to a North Vietnamese armored column today without a fight, according to military intelligence sources. And the North Vietnamese troops are now advancing toward Da Nang, the government bastion in upper South Vietnam. American planes and ships are converging on Da Nang to begin the evacuation of 1 million persons to safety. Communist gunners loosed a barrage of 14 rockets at Da Nang Air Base that left six dead and 34 wounded, mostly civilians.

Simpson's Leader-Times, Kittanning, Pennsylvania,
Wednesday, March 26, 1975

Due to the situation in Vietnam, most of the crew had pretty much written off the possibility of a Hong Kong port call, but there we were, having the experience all WestPac sailors dream about for its unmatched natural beauty and material luxury. My fellow Ensign Jim Farrens and I threw ourselves into a full day that included a guided tour of Hong Kong Island, a long lunch at one of the floating restaurants in the teeming port of Aberdeen on the island's far side, and an expensive drink at the magnificent Peninsula Hotel in Kowloon. It was thrilling to look down from Victoria Peak and see the spectacular vista of the vibrant city. We could see our own ship riding at its mooring, surrounded by numerous ferries and flotillas of junks, many with their distinctive red colored, Chinese-rigged sails.

On our tour of the city, I asked our chatty young lady tour guide if people were starting to get concerned about the return of Hong Kong to China in 1997, which was still twenty-two years in the distant future. Her well-practiced reply, chosen to amuse her customers, was, "Only the tourists, sir." I wonder if that pat answer was still being used two decades later when the grim reality was finally about to sink in. We now know that China's authoritative rule of Hong Kong is clearly not what the citizens had been promised.

Our second guided tour began with a boat ride to densely populated Lantau Island with its notorious open sewers and teeming slums, but also the vibrant energy of its bustling markets. The tour also included a bus ride on the mainland out to the "New Territories." We were taken to a vantage point from which we could look out into the vastness and unknowability of Communist China itself. One might suspect that Hong Kong slum dwellers who were not beneficiaries of the economic boom and cosmopolitan life of the colony may have seen the coming of Chinese rule as a little more attractive.

I also did some exploring on my own, which included a visit to the Royal Meteorological Office's detachment at the colony's Observatory, where I picked up a souvenir weather chart of that day's weather (which was thankfully quite benign for our entire visit). In chatting with the staff there, I learned that the founder of the U.K.'s Royal Met Office in 1854 was Vice Admiral Robert FitzRoy, and it was that naval officer who, earlier in his career, had served as the commander of the exploration ship *HMS Beagle* during Charles Darwin's famous voyage of discovery. I also discovered FitzRoy strongly disagreed with Darwin on the latter's thesis of natural selection and evolution, and, after publishing these sentiments, he and Darwin never spoke to each other again.

Back aboard ship, the junior officers who had received new job assignments were starting to get comfortable with their responsibilities. Having completed my initial assignment as first lieutenant, my job as antisubmarine warfare officer (ASWO) was to begin immediately upon our return to Pearl Harbor when Dave Rau left for his next assignment. But as I'd already managed the Pre-Overhaul Test & Inspection, my reward for having done that job well was the arrival of several boxes of paper delivered to my stateroom while I was out enjoying Hong Kong. When I opened them up, I flashed back to being handed thousands of pages of Indian Ocean weather observations back in graduate school. This new stack of paper, if piled all together, would *again* be about ten feet high. This was the "ship's force work package" for the overhaul, a nightmarishly long list of individual repair work which our own crew would do alongside the shipyard's work force when we got home.

By all appearances, my replacement as first lieutenant was my fellow Ensign and roommate Roger Wilson, who was perfect for the job; he was a former enlisted man with a personality as smooth as a barnacle-encrusted pier piling, which should have made him very well suited to lead the Bos'n mates. Roger lacked both tact and finesse, neither of which mattered much in his new job. But our visit to Hong Kong also proved he also lacked luck.

On the Saturday before Easter, the gig crew had taken the captain ashore, and since they were told to await his return in a couple of hours, they had tied the boat up at the fleet landing's pier and gone into a club for something to eat and drink. When they came back a short time later, they were horrified to find the boat – the captain's pride and joy – half submerged and literally hanging in the water by its two mooring lines. The salt water intake hose for cooling the diesel engine had come off of its fitting, allowing seawater to flood the boat. Had the boat's crew left someone there to keep watch, the flooding would have been noticed and they could have done a quick repair. But the crew – and in particular poor Roger who was still new in his job – got some verbal wire-brushing by the weapons department head Lieutenant Rick Buttina, by the executive officer Pete Finch, and of course by Captain Hekman himself.

On that same Saturday, I took a day of liberty all alone – something that's forbidden in today's Navy, even for officers, due to the threat of international terrorism. From our fleet landing, I made my way to the nearby Star Ferry and crossed to Kowloon. Since it was near noon, I found a pub where I enjoyed a simple meal of bangers and mash with a dark ale, my first introduction to traditional British fare.

Satiated, I continued my casual stroll up the main street of Kowloon and noted on a building ahead a huge poster with the image of the ever suave Roger Moore standing with crossed arms, a gun in his hand, and the beautiful, bikini-clad Britt Ekland to his side. It was a huge billboard advertising "The Man With the Golden Gun," the newly released ninth James Bond movie. And it was showing in the theater whose entrance was directly below the poster.

With several hours of free time still ahead of me, I bought a ticket and lost myself in the film, shown in English with Chinese subtitles. I've always been a fan of James Bond movies, but what made the experience extra cool was that much of the movie had been shot right there in Hong Kong and Kowloon. In fact, in one scene, "Commander Bond" enjoyed his usual innuendo-laced banter with the not-quite-dressed young woman who served his shaken-not-stirred vodka martini at a Kowloon night club called the Bottoms Up Club. The name of the club was derived from the small round bars within which attractive female bartenders served customers on hands and knees as they knelt on raised cushions in the center. After the movie, I set out in search of the club, quickly found it, and enjoyed my very own personal James Bond fantasy, and it was far better than my breathtaking experience of reading *Doctor No* as a teen-ager!

Fantasy is all well and good, of course, but what a person really remembers most vividly are the very real, very unlikely, and very intimate encounters we're so rarely treated to in life. Such a thing happened to me there in Hong Kong. On Easter Sunday, a miracle happened, as vivid and inconceivable today as it was in 1975.

After my thoroughly enjoyable day of "Bonding," I returned to the ship and hit the sack early. I had to rise very early on Easter Sunday morning to serve as officer of the deck for the 0400 to 0800 morning watch. The OOD and a petty officer of the watch were the only two watch standers on the ship's in-port quarterdeck, a ceremonial station near the stern on the starboard side of the ship – the location of the accommodation ladder (stairs) where boats would pick up or drop off passengers going ashore or coming back to the ship. The bridge was abandoned while moored, but engineering still had a watch team below keeping one boiler going and the engine room ready on fairly short notice to send power to the propellers should we require a fast getaway to sea or if our mooring line to the buoy were to break.

So there I stood on the quarterdeck with a petty officer, exchanging small talk and watching the subdued pre-dawn lights of the city across the water. Any excessively drunk or misbehaving sailors had long since been returned to the ship by the shore patrol, and all of the crew except those few standing watch, including the two of us, were sound asleep. It was, as usual, the only time on a Navy ship when things were exceptionally quiet.

Suddenly, the petty officer and I jumped at a jarring ring from the "shore phone" next to where we were standing. This was a fairly standard telephone handset hooked to a small short wave radio powered by an automobile battery. This radio-phone system was loaned to the ship by the fleet services office in Hong Kong right after we anchored and was used by visiting ships to maintain two-way communications with the pier at fleet landing. It was typically used for such things as the captain calling to have his boat sent for him, or the shore patrol asking for a boat to pick up our drunks. It was about 0530 and *nobody* would expect a call on that phone at that pre-dawn time, particularly on a Sunday/holiday morning when there would be no normal morning musters or work to be done. But on its second ring, I picked up the phone – and the miracle was on the other end.

I said, "*Stoddert* quarterdeck, officer of the deck. May I help you?" And the reply, with a voice connection that was as clear as any modern phone call, was, "Jon? Jon? Is that you?"

"Sharon? Is that you?"

The answer was yes to both!

I was stunned, as was she. Thousands of miles away, my resourceful wife had done the time zone math, simply dialed O on our home phone in Hawaii, and asked the operator if it was possible to be connected to a U.S. Navy ship in port at Hong Kong. After no small amount of time patiently waiting through various operators passing her off, clicks and hisses, she was told to stand by as the call was going through. On a ship that literally bristled with high powered radios, mostly shut down in port, we had nothing more than a little battery powered radio and telephone handset, and she'd found it. And me. In a crew of over three hundred and fifty men, it was I who answered the phone.

Sharon had been terribly lonely – enough to accept what would be a horrendously expensive phone bill charge – and figured I would surely be on board asleep on a Sunday morning. And if she could reach the ship, she reasoned they could go fetch me to come to the phone for a surprise "Happy Easter" call.

She and I, equally amazed, had a short, joyful phone conversation. I don't remember what we actually talked about – probably not the James Bond movie or the Bottom's Up Club – but what a way to celebrate

Easter! A few hours later, after getting off watch and enjoying breakfast, I went ashore one last time to find a church to attend Easter Sunday mass. I had that day, and still have today, so much to be thankful to God for.

All good things must come to an end, though. After that remarkable port visit, we were soon underway and on our way back to Subic Bay. With our radios back in service monitoring what was happening in WestPac, it was clearer than ever that the fall of the Republic of Vietnam was inevitable.

PART THREE:
This Is the End

Vietnam in 1974

CHAPTER 14

Pins and Needles

WASHINGTON – Ford Administration decisions on the amount of military aid to South Vietnam probably will depend on how effectively the Saigon government establishes a new defense perimeter.

Secretary of Defense James R. Schlesinger said, "Any question of the putting in of additional equipment into Vietnam would be based upon what we perceive to be the present needs of the situation, reflecting the possibility of a defense perimeter north of Saigon."

The Post-Crescent, Appleton, Wisconsin, Thursday, April 3, 1975

As April arrived, there wasn't any correlation between the "present needs of the situation" and the delivery of more funding for "additional equipment." The situation was dire, but those controlling the country's purse strings – meaning Congress – would have none of it. Ambassador Graham Martin was adamant that the situation, although incredibly bleak, wasn't hopeless. He held the firm belief that if the Thieu government could just get more assistance, they could successfully defend Saigon long enough to negotiate some kind of favorable peace agreement. One has to wonder what he thought would happen in the long run with a defense perimeter around the city and the rest of the country in Communist control. Nevertheless, he began personally calling friends on Capitol Hill asking for their support. And on April 15, Secretary of State Henry Kissinger went to the Senate Appropriations Committee to press for the president's request of $700 million in supplemental aid so that the Saigon government could negotiate with the Communists from a position of strength. General Fred Weyand, the last American commander on the ground in Vietnam, had argued successfully with his superiors, Ambassador Martin and Secretary Kissinger, that fresh forces could be recruited and armed in time to stabilize the situation.

But the situation wasn't any more likely to be stabilized than the U.S. Congress was to provide more funds. The Administration's efforts to shift the blame for an outright loss in Vietnam to the Congress by their failing to provide additional funding became moot. The game was over, and there was plenty of blame to go around. No additional funds were appropriated and an evacuation was inevitable. All that was left was the task of getting the losing team off the field before the stands of the winning team emptied onto it and chaos would ensue. But the question was: who, among the Vietnamese that had worked with the Americans, would be considered important enough team members to be escorted off the field and saved from the chaos?

Finding ourselves again tied up to the destroyer pier at Subic, we thought it was inevitable that ships of the Seventh Fleet would be mobilized to support whatever the evacuation plans were to be. Much has been written about the options that were presented to the President and about the final execution of what became known as "Option 4." Operation Frequent Wind was its code name, but on our ship, except for perhaps the captain, XO, and operations officer, we knew very little. Letters home to loved ones weren't very substantive since we could only speculate. And I did just that. I hand-wrote a letter to Sharon on a notepad while on watch again as officer of the deck, standing on the quarterdeck in the middle of the night. It was just the petty officer of the watch (POOW) and me, welcoming all the drunks coming back aboard (some, as always, delivered by the Shore Patrol). The POOW and I shared the 0000 to 0400 watch with a handful of other watch standers down in the engineering plant and two roving patrols, one for security and one to check water and fuel levels in various tanks and the bilge. With pretty much nothing to do, but much on my mind, here's what I wrote, and succeeded in getting off the ship in the outgoing mail that morning.

2:30 AM Saturday, April 5

Sharon, my Wife,

I'm writing this as I stand my OOD watch in Subic Bay. If I didn't have duty with everyone ashore I would have gotten off to call you tonight. The reason is that I want to warn you of a possible, more likely probable, lapse in mail from me in the next few weeks.

Tonight at 10 PM we received word that we are to get underway tomorrow, mission and destination undetermined. The crew knows nothing of it and I don't really know why or where to. I just want to warn you that it's more than possible that this could involve the Stoddert in the evacuation efforts of Da Nang, Saigon, or Phnom Penh. I don't mean to frighten you and I've considered my wording so as to not to. The days of active involvement of the U.S. military in SE Asia are over. It's a sad state that those countries will certainly fall and after the tremendous loss of life and resources and the reputation of our country. It's sickening. But anyway, U.S. warships are being used to protect the rescue ships actually doing the evacuation. They aren't any nearer [to the coast] than the horizon. And it's obvious now that at least for us, the fighting's over. I just pity those god forsaken countries.

So Sharon, keep in touch with the other wives. Some of the husbands may know more than I do and may have gotten some details home but I doubt it.

This could all be for nothing and I pray that's true. There's a possibility of Danger, but I doubt it. There is a possibility (very vague) that this could mean a change in our return date. I wish I had more answers Sharon but I don't.

I want you to keep your chin up and getting tanned for me. Chances are this is another Navy game. I'll be glad when I'm through being a pawn in a game played by fools.

I'll write as soon as I can get a letter off. Don't worry Sharon, your love is with me.

And mine with you.
Jon

"I'll be glad when I'm through being a pawn in a game played by fools." How interesting that I'd have actually written those words. I'd written them somewhere in the four hour stint of that watch, all spent standing up, in the wee hours of the morning after having had no more than a few hours of sleep before going on watch. In those words, I guess I captured all the uncertainty of what our role would be, if any, in the final days of Vietnam, and all my frustration at having been away from my wife and home. It all leaked out in that one sentence. I knew with certainty, however, that after months of sailing all over the western Pacific and Indian Ocean with zero involvement with anything to do with Vietnam, we were on our way to an uncertain role that would be set against the absolutely certain outcome of the war. In spite of my well-trained ability to keep my personal opinions about how naval forces are employed to myself, I succumbed to summing up the whole Vietnam experience as a game, and my Navy career as having been run "by fools." Such was my state of mind that night.

It was very fortunate I actually got that letter off the ship. It went into the last mail bag that was handed ashore at 0800. The "special sea and anchor detail" was set sometime around 0700 and we got underway at 0829. Our destination: Vietnam.

CHAPTER 15

Welcome to Vietnam

SAIGON (UPI) - South Vietnamese government forces made their first significant counterattack against massive Communist advances today, moving back into the abandoned city of Nha Trang, 188 miles northeast of Saigon... More American civilians fled Saigon in what was the beginning of a U.S. exodus. Hundreds of Vietnamese war orphans left by plane for the United States, but military orders closed the city to virtually all other Vietnamese.

The Sunday Valley News, Van Nuys, California, Sunday, April 6, 1975

On Sunday, April 6, we steamed toward South Vietnam in company with our sister ship, the *USS Cochrane (DDG-21).* In the late morning, we slowed together in order to allow the *Cochrane's* chaplain to be transferred by boat to our ship for an interdenominational service which was held on the fantail area, the largest open area on our ship's deck. While I don't remember anything the chaplain said, I can well imagine it was a much-needed prayer for the people of Vietnam and for the safety of our crew on this mission.

Unfortunately, there were never enough chaplains in the Navy to have one on every ship, so after transferring him back to *Cochrane,* the two ships parted company en route to our assigned holding stations, ours being off the coast near the Saigon River at Vung Tau.

At 0800 on Monday, April 7, Lieutenant (JG) Mike Vanderpool and I went on watch as OOD and JOOD. When Mike took the deck and I took the conn, we were twenty-seven and a half nautical miles from the closest point of land, which was the coast of South Vietnam. Our ship was alone, unaccompanied by any other Navy ships, and we steamed at a fuel-conserving speed of five knots toward an assigned station near Vung Tau, a peninsula just over forty miles southeast of Saigon, where American naval forces were being gathered to do nobody-knew-what. I detected an energy level on the bridge that was new and different. We'd been told we'd soon cross to within twelve statute miles of the coast, officially putting us in a war zone. Word spread quickly through the ship that spending even a day inside that perimeter would mean our pay would be tax-exempt for the entire month, with a supplemental hazardous duty pay bonus, and we could mail our letters home without stamps. We were all so poor that even getting a few extra bucks was pretty exciting—in spite of the intangible potential costs. But the other buzz that morning was that we and our ship were almost back to Vietnam, which meant those of us who had not previously fought in the war, either on the gun line or onshore, were about to become Vietnam veterans.

About mid-morning during our watch, we could clearly make out the coast of Vietnam off our bow. The visibility was excellent and we could see the land from about fifteen nautical miles away as a line of green hills. On the bridge, Mike and I trained our binoculars on the mythical place that had dominated the news for most of our adult lives. Even though we were still in international waters, we were *there.*

Then, at 1048, just inside thirteen nautical miles from shore, a lifeless body floated past the ship on the port side. Our navigator, Jim

Farrens, who was on the bridge at the time, was the first to see it. He was looking down from the port bridge wing watching poisonous black and white sea snakes swimming on the surface and yelled out "Hey, that's a body!" Mike and I ran to the port side bridge wing, arriving just in time to see it passing down the side, about 50 feet away. I had the conn and, with a nod from Mike, I gave the engine and rudders orders we had practiced many times to use for a man overboard. Having reversed our course, we slowly drifted to a stop with the body just off the port beam. Even from this distance, we could see that it was probably a male with short dark hair, face down, and dressed in what looked like a green uniform.

Captain Hekman, whom we had called as we made our maneuvers, arrived on the bridge and gave orders that we were to recover the body, attempt to identify him, and convey this information to higher authority.

The Bos'n Mates had already anticipated what was going to happen and hustled to man up the motor whaleboat and prepare to lower it into the water. The sea was very calm, with almost no wind, so what was normally a dangerous operation would be swift and safe. I expected that our new First Lieutenant Roger Wilson would be in charge of the boat going out to retrieve the body, but suddenly, the captain turned to me and said, "Jon, you go. Take charge of the boat." My adrenaline spiked, and I fired back, "Aye aye, sir."

Arriving at the whaleboat, which hung from its davits on the port side, I saw Roger and said, "Sorry, but I'm the JOOD and the CO told me to be boat officer." To his great credit, he just said "OK" and stepped back. I suspected he felt the same way I did; that this would be anything but pleasant.

In the boat with me, all of us in kapok life jackets and plastic safety helmets, were Bos'n Mates first class Charlie Ferris, second class Mike

Lucci, and third class Frankie Taranovich, along with an engineman and one other seaman. Those petty officers, who had been working for me for the past five months, were men I knew to be total professionals. As the boat was lowered into the sea and the lines cast off, we were initially very quiet, and then, as we approached the body, somebody said, "Do you think it could be booby-trapped?" I suspected we were all thinking about this. Ferris said, "There's only one way to find out." We stopped with the body next to our starboard side. Using a long boat hook, one of the men reached down and turned him over while we all held our breath. What we saw was horrible.

The poor man had no face and no fingers. He had clearly been in the sea for several days – three to be exact, we later learned – and the sea life mafia had done their best to remove his identity. We recognized his uniform as that of a U.S. Air Force flight suit, with our American flag on his sleeve. The worst shock of all was the unbelievable stench of death that assaulted us. I can still smell it, if I think about it, these forty-one years later. In my 65 years, it's the only time, thank God, that I ever experienced the smell of a decomposing human body. My heart goes out to those whose professions require such exposure. I couldn't help but wonder who this person was, not to mention the circumstances surrounding his death.

We had brought with us a heavy rubberized body bag, personally delivered to the boat by our supply officer Roger MacInnis. It was the first one I'd ever seen, and the thought went through my head that I had no idea where we stored them on the ship, and that I had never even considered such an item would be part of our supplies. But, of course it was. There was no time for such thoughts, though – we *really* needed to get him inside an air-tight bag, and quickly. After we unfolded and unzipped the bag we had to pull the airman aboard. It took three of the sailors using all their strength to haul the body – he was a physically big man – into the boat. Thankfully, his flight suit had not decayed enough to make it too weak to be used to get a grip on him. As he was clumsily slid into the body bag, Ferris retrieved his wallet from a back pocket and handed it to me. We hadn't noticed a stitched name tag on his chest, so we didn't yet have a name. We radioed the ship that we were recovering a U.S. Air Force service member and motored back to the ship.

I returned to the bridge with the wallet, and the bag was stowed in one of our food refrigerators (something we tried, unsuccessfully, to not think about for the next several days). A couple of the sailors directed to handle the body bag simply couldn't force themselves to do it because the seal on the bag wasn't complete due to the man's large size, and the stench was overpowering. So replacement volunteers were quickly found and the job done. Up on the bridge, from his Air Force ID card, we identified the airman as Staff Sergeant Donald Thomas Dionne, Sr. His name and social security number were recorded in the deck log, which also noted I took the conn back at 1130. That whole evolution, from sighting the body to his recovery and setting off again toward the coast, had taken only forty minutes. But those were forty minutes that I, for one, have never forgotten.

As our watch ended, Mike and I turned over the bridge to Pete Coste and Jim Farrens. I went down to my stateroom, put every stitch of my clothing in a plastic bag until I could get them to the ship's laundry, took a *long* hot shower (normally a forbidden waste of precious fresh water needed for the boilers), dressed in a clean uniform, and went to lunch. I seem to remember not being very hungry because: (a) the memory of such a morbid sight and stench were still too fresh, and (b) I also knew Sergeant Dionne was in the chill box with the food we'd be eating. My fellow officers seemed to show me a little deference, not saying much to me. In fact, I didn't say much of anything at all for a couple of hours. After pushing my food around, I retreated to my stateroom and immersed myself in the overhaul work package paperwork.

The U.S. Naval command in Saigon gave us instructions to await a helicopter that would retrieve the airman. In mid-afternoon when the helo arrived overhead, I grabbed my camera and went topside in time to see it was a silver-painted Huey. On its fuselage was the painted name "Air America," which was well known to be the quasi-commercial company operated by the CIA. Our helo deck was small and configured for hover-only, and so our deceased airman, who had been retrieved from his short stay in cold storage, was lifted up about thirty feet by a cable and then pulled into the hovering aircraft, which then promptly rose and departed in the direction from which it had come: Saigon. I managed to get a couple of clear pictures of the chopper and the basket with the airman being lifted from our deck. As the aircraft flew away, I realized we hadn't done anything such as muster an honor guard to salute him as he left the ship. Looking back now, I regret we hadn't done more to show respect for this American service member who had given his life while conducting a humanitarian mission.

It turned out that Staff Sergeant Dionne was a crewmember from a U.S. Air Force C-5A Galaxy transport plane. He was a thirty year old flight engineer from Van Nuys, California who had left behind his wife, two sons, and a daughter. Today, he rests in peace in Arlington National Cemetery, and his name is on the wall of the Vietnam Veterans Memorial in Washington. But how he ended up floating in the water about thirteen miles off the coast of Vietnam, and what happened to that aircraft, is worth noting.

In South Vietnam, there were a number of orphanages taking care of hundreds of babies and young children, many of whom had been fathered by Americans while stationed there. In March and early April, Sister Susan Carol McDonald of the Sisters of Loretto was on the staff of one of those orphanages. In her memoirs published later, she wrote about how disheartening it was, during those weeks, to see commercial aircraft fly overhead filled to capacity with Americans and Vietnamese who had been working for U.S. agencies, flying away from danger and toward security and hope. She knew plans had been drawn up for the children in her care to be evacuated and adopted by families in the United States, but there hadn't yet been any action taken. With the situation in the country deteriorating fast, it was clear to her that if the American staff was withdrawn and these children weren't able to leave the country, it meant death was a distinctly possible outcome for them. This was truly a dire situation.

There were organizations in the States, like the U.S. Agency for International Development (USAID), already working to resolve this situation and address other associated humanitarian concerns. President Ford had taken a personal interest in this matter and his Administration named the effort to evacuate the orphans "Operation Baby Lift." On April 3, the sisters were notified that three Medivac aircraft, charter flights contracted with World Airways, were waiting in the Philippines and would arrive the next day to begin transporting the children out. However, on the following day they were told that USAID now believed the charter flights would be too dangerous for the children, and instead, a U.S. Air Force C-5A Galaxy would be provided, one of the world's largest aircraft that had just been put into service. Perhaps this was due to the personal attention of President Ford. The Galaxy had landed at Tan Son Nhut Airbase just outside of Saigon and was unloading what may have been the very last shipment of military supplies, probably artillery and ammunition, for the hard-pressed Republic of Vietnam Army. With the giant military airplane now empty and ready to fly out, the orphanages were told to move quickly and transport their children to the airport to put them aboard.

At the same time, Sharon and other *Stoddert* wives in Honolulu had volunteered to stand by at Hickam Air Force Base to assist the nurses and other officials in caring for the children after they arrived. Help would be needed to re-embark the children on flights that would take them onward to the mainland, or to provide temporary care while awaiting later flights.

Back at the airbase, Sister McDonald and the other care-providers had to make gut wrenching decisions about which children to send. Because it was a military aircraft without the comforts of a commercial jetliner, the conditions on board would be Spartan. With so many children in her care, she made the decision to send the oldest toddlers and only 22 of the strongest infants who could be strapped into seats in the troop compartment of the aircraft. She decided to hold back the high risk babies.

After the children were taken on board the aircraft and the doors closed, the crew reportedly experienced some difficulty with the rear cargo hatch, a problem they had previously noted. With the hatch apparently closed securely, the aircraft then taxied for departure with what was initially reported to be 305 souls aboard, of which 243 were children, 44 were escorts either from the orphanages or military bases, 16 crewmembers, and 2 flight nurses. A later report, however, had this total higher, at 328 people, with the additional passengers probably being U.S. nationals, desperate to leave Vietnam, who talked their way on board at the air base. At the controls were Air Force Captain Dennis "Bud" Traynor and co-pilot Captain Tilford Harp. With its four very powerful General Electric turbofan engines, each capable of 43,000 pounds of force (thrust), the 222 foot wingspan lifted the 247 foot long behemoth into the tropical air and began to ascend to its planned altitude of 31,000 feet.

But this mission of mercy turned into unfathomable tragedy. As the aircraft cleared the coast on the most direct path to international air space by flying south, it turned to a southeasterly heading of 136 degrees, directly toward Clark Airbase in the Philippines. Then the unthinkable happened. Still climbing past 23,000 feet, the cargo door in the rear of the aircraft opened explosively, causing an instantaneous decompression of the cabin, filling the plane with mist and debris. The cargo hatch and Staff Sergeant Dionne fell to the sea far below. The massive trauma of the explosion had severed control cables to the rudder and elevator on the plane's huge tail, causing the failure of two of the four hydraulic systems, leaving the pilot with almost complete lack of flight control.

Captains Traynor and Harp instantly fought to maintain control of the plane. Having use of only one aileron, the spoilers, and control of power to the engines, they executed what was later called a heroic effort. They managed to turn the aircraft around and radioed in for an emergency approach to Tan Son Nhut, which was, at that time, about fifty miles away. Unable to control the rate of descent, they plunged rapidly and still almost made it to the airport. Almost. In a turn to make their final approach, they added power to offset their too-rapid descent but it wasn't enough. At 4:45 pm, the plane hit the ground in a rice paddy, skidded a short distance, became airborne for another half mile crossing the Saigon River, and then hit a dike, breaking up into several pieces, and was quickly engulfed in fire from burning fuel. The crash site was over a mile from the nearest road, slowing the arrival of relief and firefighting equipment. That there were any survivors at all was miraculous. And, to illustrate the difficulty of the recovery effort, the location had been the site of an engagement with the Viet Cong as recently as the previous night.

In this nightmare, those who lost their lives included 76 children, 34 Defense Attaché personnel, five civilian dependents, 11 Air Force service members, and eight nurses from other countries. There were 175 survivors and all of the orphans among them were later flown to the United States on other aircraft. Among the dead was twenty-seven year old Air Force Captain Mary Therese Klinker, the last U.S. nurse to die in the Vietnam War. Her name is engraved on the Vietnam Veterans Memorial in Washington immediately to the right of Staff Sergeant Dionne's name. These Americans, along with the other military casualties of that tragic flight, were among the last to die in the Vietnam War.

What of the aircraft itself? The huge C-5A Galaxy, the newest asset in the U.S. Air Force fleet, had gone through a difficult birthing. The plane, intended for global airlift capable of moving massive amounts of equipment and very large components such as helicopters and armored vehicles, was designed and built by Lockheed Corporation in Marietta, Georgia. Lockheed had won the contract award for the heavy-lifter over a higher-cost Boeing design in September, 1965. The program experienced huge cost over-runs, went through two Congressional investigations, and narrowly survived threats of termination of the contract. It was reportedly saved only by the promise of a large order for the planes from the government of Iran, which was at that time still under the leadership of Shah Mohammad Reza Pahlavi. That Iranian order was never placed, but the C-5A went into production anyway and entered operational service in 1970. The crash in Vietnam put a new spotlight on Lockheed and the program, resulting in an intense inquiry by the Air Force to understand what had happened and why. Had the plane been sabotaged before the flight, or was it caused by human error aboard the aircraft? Wreckage from the crash site was eventually collected in spite of looting, mostly because the Air Force paid rewards to the local populace if they found, or returned from early pilfering, parts from the plane. The all-important flight recorder was recovered from the crash site, but another critical piece of evidence was the cargo hatch itself, which had blown out over the sea and was seemingly irretrievable. The *USS Benjamin Stoddert* later had an opportunity to take part in the search for the hatch.

The service's Accident Investigation Board found the likely reason there had been any survivors at all was Captain Traynor's use of engine power to maintain some control and his decision to crash land while he still could. Both the pilot and co-pilot were later awarded the highly prestigious Air Force Cross for their skill and heroism. After the inquiry there was a lawsuit between the Government and Lockheed regarding alleged problems with the company's design and workmanship. But the C-5 Galaxy fleet of aircraft was eventually cleared for continued operation and, with evolutionary modifications and improvements, continues in active Air Force service today.

With our unsettling arrival at Vietnam over with, *Stoddert* was assigned to a small holding sector, patrolling the coast just within sight of the village of Vung Tau. Before the war, Vung Tau had been a resort area with beautiful beaches and luxurious accommodations. As I've been told, even as the war raged, Vung Tau was sort of a refuge for peaceful recreation and relaxation for well-heeled visitors from *both* north and south. It was the site of a massive statue of Jesus, called "Christ the King of Vung Tau," which had just been built in 1974. Reaching to a height of 118 feet with two outstretched arms 60 feet wide, it was a magnificent sight even through our binoculars from offshore. And it was certainly ironic, considering the circumstances.

For us, however, Vung Tau was simply a peninsula down river from Saigon and the location to which we were sent, along with several other ships from Task Force 76. Having been assigned a patrol box to remain within, called a "Gator Box" since this kind of offshore loitering was common to amphibious ships, we began to roll a dice to determine which of the six charted points within the sector we would head to next. During periods of release from that sector, we often lazily circled the Task Force flagship *USS Blue Ridge* and through our binoculars watched the Marines practice running into helicopters on deck and then running out of the helicopters in mock assaults. They did this for what seemed like hundreds of times. But maybe it seemed that way because of the many, many circles we sailed in random patrols around the flagship, and back in our "Gator Box," as other ships of the fleet patrolled their own assigned areas of nautical purgatory.

This went on for day after sweltering day as we monitored the news from Saigon. Our crew worked through the tedium of shipboard life, while living with the uncertainty of what was happening twenty miles away in Saigon, or thousands of miles away at home. We were cut off from nearly all contact with our loved ones except for periodic deliveries of sacks of mail for which we either sent our whaleboat to the flagship to retrieve or received lowered from helicopters hovering over our stern.

CHAPTER 16

Time for Reflection

SAIGON, South Vietnam (AP) – A camouflaged jet warplane of the South Vietnamese air force bombed the downtown palace of President Nguyen Van Thieu Tuesday, shattering windows in the modern four-story building.

Witnesses said the U.S.-made F5 swooped in at a 2,000 foot level over the palace and dropped at least two and possibly four 500-pound bombs.

Thieu and his family were not injured but palace sources said two persons were killed and three were wounded. It was not known if the victims were in the palace or surrounding gardens.

Three hours after the bombing, Thieu made a radio address to the nation saying the attack was not a coup and he still had the support of the armed forces.

He said, "This morning at 8:30 a.m., an F5 jet of the South Vietnamese air force bombed the presidential palace but I and my family are safe. I and the vice president are still working together with the armed forces." Thieu then added, "I am determined to continue my leadership of this country."

The Post-Standard, Syracuse, New York, Tuesday, April 8, 1975

Our routine of low speed loitering in holding areas off Vung Tau went on for two weeks, and, as I said, it had become painfully tedious. We could see the high terrain above Vung Tau in the distance through the haze, but mostly we saw other U.S. Navy ships. Occasionally, a black and white ringed sea snake would drift by. These poisonous creatures, related to venomous terrestrial snakes found in Australia, live only at sea and, lacking gills, need to surface periodically to breathe. Seeing one would usually elicit a comment by someone that we wouldn't want to be swimming with them. The weather was unremarkable; very hot and humid. As had been the case ever since we left Taiwan and headed south to the Philippines and Indian Ocean, our enlisted men were absolved from wearing their blue chambray working uniform shirts and went about their work in white tee shirts and dungarees. We officers and chief petty officers stayed in our short sleeved khaki shirts and matching long trousers, although we'd heard of some ships where the wearing of shorts had been authorized. Captain Hekman placed great stock in professional appearance, and his wardroom and the Chiefs' mess followed his lead.

We stood our watches, ate our meals, and kept up the ship's maintenance. And even though we drilled at general quarters at least once a day, we were denied the satisfaction of test firing the guns, launching missiles, or shooting torpedoes. Our most "warlike" exercise was the periodic firing of small arms from the fantail. But popping off pistol shots into a target-less sea (except for the opportunity to try to hit one of those sea snakes) was pretty unexciting.

Throughout that time at sea, I was still working my way through the several foot deep stack of pre-overhaul paperwork. I was also thinking a lot about our return home, of my chance to see and hold Sharon again, and about our future. I had come to my tour on *Stoddert* with simple goals in mind. I was trying to do the best I could at my job in order to hopefully get top-of-the-heap fitness reports, which could earn me a strong recommendation for my transfer out of "unrestricted line" duty and into the "restricted line" officer corps for meteorologists and oceanographers. I had applied for this "Geophysics Special Duty" designation while attending the Naval Postgraduate School a year earlier, but had been turned down because of the requirement for three years of fleet experience. The Navy had been unwilling to waive this for me, so here I was with one year down and two more to go before I could re-apply, and then embark on the rest of my career as a specialist in the environmental sciences. Meanwhile, there we were, floating listlessly in the South China Sea.

But my wife and my career weren't the only things I was thinking about. I had become a Vietnam serviceman, the one thing I had truly hoped to avoid as a teenager. I had high school classmates and neighborhood friends from the North Shore get sent to Vietnam. To the best of my knowledge, all of the guys I knew had come back in one piece, but, of course, they had been forever changed by the experience. Many members of the *Stoddert* crew, those with more years of service than I, had been there before too. They had been on destroyers or other ships on the gun line along the coast, or on small boats up in the Mekong Delta, or they had served on aircraft carriers supporting the air war over Vietnam. Our new chief engineer, Lieutenant Don Colley, had been an advisor to the South Vietnamese Navy in the delta. In other words, *Stoddert* was home to quite a few Vietnam veterans, and "my time in 'Nam" was long overdue.

Back at St. John's Prep, as soon as I knew I was accepted to the Naval Academy, I also knew I'd never be drafted into the Army. This gave me a huge sense of relief in addition to my excitement to have been offered a chance to attend the Academy – and get a free college education. The choice between the Academy's rigor and getting shot at in the jungle was an easy one. And I remember my dad's not too subtle hints that Navy life was much better than Army life.

Given that ALL of Representative William Bates' nominees actually went to the military academies, assuming they accepted their nominations and were physical qualified, my two alternates, Steve Lalonde of

Marblehead and Jüergen "Yogi" Saggerer of Salem, also accepted their nominations. We were all told to show up on July 1 for induction day into the Class of 1973. I already knew Steve because he'd graduated from my same high school a year earlier and was in a military prep school. He'd been my football teammate and our star quarterback, taking us to the 1967 Catholic Conference and State Championships. Yogi attended nearby Salem High School and we met each other at a track meet in Andover, Massachusetts while competing against each other on our respective schools' teams. Unlike Steve, I wasn't a star football player. I was the second string fullback who had to watch from the bench while our starting fullback, a 220 pound converted lineman named George Spartichino, easily pounded his way through the opposing teams' lines. On the Prep track team, I wasn't fast enough to be a top notch sprinter nor tall and lean enough to run the high hurdles very well, but my skills found a good home in the 180 yard intermediate hurdles and the long jump, and I loved to throw the javelin. I don't remember what events Yogi ran, but as soon as we met each other, it was obvious we were both thrilled to be going to the Naval Academy.

Let me share a side note about the gentleman who offered the three of us this life-changing opportunity. Congressman Bates of Salem had himself served as a Navy officer after graduating from Brown University in 1940 and receiving an officer's commission. His father, George J. Bates, had been a multiple-term member of Congress until his death in a tragic plane crash at Washington National Airport in 1949. William (or Bill to his friends, which included my future parents in law who had attended Salem High with him!) resigned his commission to take his dad's seat in Congress, and was re-elected several times, serving until his own death due to cancer in June of 1969. Steve, Yogi, and I all attended his funeral in Salem together, just one week before we reported to the Academy.

I should add that in his honor, the Navy named a *Sturgeon*-class nuclear attack submarine the *USS Willam H. Bates (SSN-680),* which was commissioned on May 5, 1973. That date was exactly one month and a day before my classmates and I were commissioned officers at the Naval Academy on June 6. The *Bates* was originally planned to be named the *USS Redfish,* but in a break with tradition, she was named instead after the deceased and highly admired Congressman by Secretary of the Navy John Chafee. In response to criticism from traditionalists who wanted to continue the longstanding practice of naming attack submarines after fish, Admiral Hyman Rickover, who at that time led the Navy nuclear propulsion program, responded with a terse statement of the obvious: "Fish don't vote!" That quote, characteristic of the acerbic Admiral Rickover, soon became famous in Navy circles.

Steve, Yogi, and I were very lucky to have been hand-picked by such a distinguished political leader. But, surprisingly, both of my friends left the Academy before the point of no return at the end of our second year. Any mid who stays into the start of the third academic year commits himself (or now, of course, herself) to either stay until graduation or go to the fleet as an enlisted sailor. I stayed all the way through the four years there because the free education being provided by the Navy was just about the best thing ever to have happened to me up to that point in my life. My parents were of very modest means and, unlike my two big brothers who had won football scholarships to Tufts University, I was simply not going to get a football scholarship, nor was I able to afford to go college, except maybe an in-state school such as the University of Massachusetts, to which I'd also been offered admittance. Staying at USNA was the only option I saw for myself. But what was on my mind, and almost certainly on the mind of my classmates who stayed and those who left, and probably every healthy young man born in the late 1940's and early 1950's, was Vietnam.

Most young men of our generation were subject to the draft. Vietnam was sucking in, chewing up, and spitting out draftees by the thousands, and the three of us Malay boys could have been among them. My older brothers had been passed over by the draft not because of academic deferments, but based on medical disqualifications; one with an unrepaired hernia and the other with obesity, which is interesting since they both continued to play football and other sports through all four of their years at Tufts! My future brother-in-law Peter Healey and many others managed to get into ROTC programs or, as in the case of future President George W. Bush, commissions in the Air Force reserves. And then all of us waited for the draft lottery to see how we fared. Each of us led our lives overshadowed by what was about to happen when birth dates were drawn in Washington, guaranteeing military service to those with low numbers, whether they liked it or not.

On the morning of July 1, 1969, I reported to the Naval Academy to be inducted as a Midshipman and began the sweaty, exhausting, and stress-filled experience known as Plebe Summer. Almost immediately, I had my head shaved and was issued uniforms and everything I needed as a Plebe, right down to shaving cream and deodorant. (The smell of Gillette Foamy shave cream still takes me back to that summer!) And I started to get yelled at *a lot*. Thus began what became the rest of my life. And, ironically, on that very same day the U.S. Government held its second draft lottery, this one for men born in 1951 – my lottery. It shouldn't have been surprising that our Plebe class suffered significant attrition due to resignations beginning that very first week and continuing throughout the summer, and then during the whole first year. Over the course of our four years, the Class of '73 lost about one out of every five of those of us young men who raised our hands on the afternoon July 1 to be sworn in as Midshipmen. On the other hand, in an address to our entire class on one of the first days of Plebe Summer, an officer told us to look to the left and then to the right of us and get it into our heads that one of those guys would be gone by the time we graduated. So at least we beat those odds!

As a brief aside, the upperclassmen assigned to train us that summer were the rising juniors, or Midshipmen Second Class (2/C), from the Class of 1971. Although I didn't think so at the time, almost all of them turned out to be really great guys as we got to know them through the rest of that academic year in 15th Company. (There were, at that time, 36 companies in the Brigade of Midshipmen, whereas today there are only 30.) For that summer, though, we were designated H ("Hotel") Company and our Company Commander was Midshipman 2/C Frank Culbertson. I mention this because, after graduation, Frank went on to become a jet pilot in the fleet, then a Navy test pilot, and eventually a NASA astronaut. He was the only American "off the planet" in 2001 when the attack on the U.S. happened on 9/11. He was flying with two Russian crewmates on the still under construction International Space Station. Frank's emotional and insightful letter, written while he looked down helplessly at the smoke rising from the World Trade Center, which he could see from space, is incredibly moving. I most highly recommend you find it and read it on nasa.gov ("Astronaut Frank Culbertson Letter from September 11, 2001.") I'm proud to say Frank remains among my professional and personal friends today and is enjoying a very successful career as a senior executive for a company that launches resupply missions to the ISS and science probes out into the solar system for NASA.

Clearly, many of those who quit during that summer did so for the practical and understandable reason that the Plebe experience sucked! Really sucked! But I believe many of those who quit had actually been waiting to see what their lottery number was, to see how likely they were to be drafted, and leave if they pulled a high enough number. I don't know where the cutoff was for my group of men, but it was safe to believe that if you had a high number, let's say, from 151 to 356, the chances of wearing a uniform unless voluntarily were pretty slim. The guys who quit for this reason experienced no draft, but they earned no Naval Academy diploma or Navy commission either. The lottery number for my July 14, 1951 birthday was 156. With that number, I would have almost certainly been safe, but with me there at the Naval Academy, it was a moot point. To be honest, I no longer cared. Even before I applied to the Academy, I had gotten my head around the possibility that by the time I graduated the war in Vietnam would still be going on, and there was a chance I'd be fighting in it. But after getting into the Academy, I also knew that unless I chose to become a Marine or go to flight school, I'd be an officer in dry clothes with hot meals on a gray ship or inside the bowels of a black nuclear submarine... pretty much the picture my dad had painted for me. This was preferable to fighting a bloody war on the ground – sitting in that dirt hole my dad warned me about – and getting shot at!

Two weeks before I was due to enter the Academy, our local newspaper, *The Beverly Times*, sent a reporter to interview me and my parents. It wasn't every day that our little town of Beverly Farms, a more or less idyllic subset of the city of Beverly nestled on the rocky coast of the North Shore, sent a kid to one of the service academies. The piece that came out on June 14 had the strangest headline: "Cadet-to-Be Says No Time To Let Things Happen." The picture of me, taken in my front yard leaning against a tree, was pretty good. But the caption beneath the picture made me choke: "ON HIS OWN: Jonathan T. Malay isn't listening to his friends who rib him about the Navy. He'll go to the Naval Academy." The text of the article was a mixture of good and horrifying. The good part came in the place I was quoted as saying this:

> "'I was looking for a career in engineering, and I decided to do something different,' he said. 'I can get the finest education possible at the academy, and get my military obligation over at the same time. There are worse ways to spend time in the military besides being an officer. It's not that I'm a masochist or anything, but I just think it will be a good life. I think I have the patience and good nature to take the military regimentation, so I'm not worried about the first year,' he said. 'There's also a lot of opportunities to do graduate work down there. It's hard to say right now if I'll make a career of the Navy. I'll have to wait until I get the feel of it. They sort of expect you to make a career of it, anyway,' he said."

Holy mackerel! Those words were about the smartest and most prescient words I think I had uttered in my entire youth up to that point. It's all pretty much exactly as it came to pass in the years that followed, right down to my going into graduate school immediately after graduating from the Academy, with the exception that I chose oceanography and meteorology over engineering, which was a minor detail.

But it's too bad I didn't stop talking there. Later in the article, the reporter wrote, "Malay has definite views about the relationship of the military to the country and the world…" And those views of mine came out in these words of wisdom:

> "I believe in patriotism, but not blindly. Sure, there's an unpopular war going on, and it's disturbing to the people. I agree it is wrong. But people who say the military is unnecessary have got to be a little sick. We've got to keep things from happening. We've got to work to maintain peace. I look at the military as an organization of people who have committed themselves to serve their country. Except the ones who are drafted, of course. Their country takes preference over everything. If it preserves world peace, fine. I wouldn't want to be drafted myself. But with a war going on it's necessary."

These were interesting and somewhat confused words to be coming from an eighteen year old kid. But I had been correctly quoted in the press as saying: "I agree it is wrong." Those true words came from both the heart and mind of the kid I was. But how would it play in Annapolis, if anyone there ever read the article? That's what I wondered as I read the newspaper on the day it was published.

And yet, there I was in Annapolis. I made it through Plebe Summer just fine. That "patience and good nature" I had described myself as having turned out to serve me well, as did the physical fitness from having just finished the spring track season at my high school, which left me in better shape than a lot of my classmates. I was smart enough to keep my mouth shut except when needed, and I worked hard to remember all the trivia Plebes are required to memorize from a pocket-size handbook called *Reef Points*, and I strained hard enough to be in the top half of all the physical fitness challenges. So, even though it sucked, I did fine as a Plebe. And my views on Vietnam were now being informed by the force-feeding of assigned newspaper reading and listening to officers who had been-there-done-that in actual combat. If I'd been inclined to think American involvement in the Vietnam War was still wrong, I sure didn't say so there at the Academy. I was on my path to becoming the strongly patriotic and yet flaming politically moderate I am today.

So there I sat in one of my classes just before the Christmas break at the end of my first academic semester. The professor was a Marine Corps officer, an excellent instructor whom I greatly admired. And on that day as class began, he pulled from his briefcase a newspaper clipping and announced to the class, "I thought you might want to see what's been hanging all semester long in my department's office here in the building. This is from *The Beverly Times* in Massachusetts and it's about Midshipman Malay here." He walked up the aisle and laid the clipping on my desk, saying to me, "We've had a little pool going in the office to see how long you were going to last here, Mr. Malay. And since you've lasted longer than all of the bets, including mine, we thought you should have this as a souvenir." To which I think I said something no more profound than, "Thank you, sir." But privately, I found it embarrassing and hilarious in equal measure.

I took that clipping back to my room in Bancroft Hall and placed it into my Plebe-issue gray metal lockbox, the ten-by-fifteen-by-six inch treasure chest a Midshipman can *privately* store pretty much anything he (and now she) wishes, since it was never required to be open for room inspections. Forty five years later, I still have that lockbox, from which I've pulled that news clipping to use in writing this chapter. It sits in front of me, and will soon go back into the box, back with my plastic engraved name plate used for every dorm room I occupied in my four years living in Bancroft Hall. The box also contains the original of Sharon's and my marriage certificate, the deed to our home of thirty years, photos of me and my brothers when we were very young, and the originals of the discharge papers from my Navy retirement back in 1993. What greater treasures could there possibly be?

As my Academy years went by, the war in Vietnam raged on with Americans fighting and dying, including Naval Academy graduates, some of whom were my own company's graduated upperclassmen. There were prisoners of war suffering in Hanoi, and the country was collectively wringing its hands through my first three years there. Then, in January of my senior year, the horror suddenly ended for the United States when the so-called Peace Accords were signed in Paris. Until then, we Midshipmen all knew our responsibility to become part of the fight was a distinct possibility. We developed our warfighting skills and prepared to do whatever was asked of us. But because of the Accords, my country had never before asked me to go to Vietnam. And yet, there off the coast in April, 1975, that call had finally come, and I was still ready to do what was necessary.

If only somebody would finally tell us what that was.

CHAPTER 17

Beginning the Ending: Operation Frequent Wind

SAIGON (AP) – North Vietnamese tanks and troops pushed eastward toward Saigon on Sunday in what one South Vietnamese general said could be the beginning of an offensive against the capital.

As tanks rolled to within 17 miles of the city, the National Assembly named retired Gen. Duong Van "Big" Minh, a neutralist, as president to replace Tran Van Huong in hopes of obtaining a negotiated settlement that would spare Saigon from a major assault...

Hundreds of South Vietnamese militiamen dropped their weapons in a pile and fled in the path of the two-pronged assault by Communist-led forces. More than 100,000 fleeing refugees also were stretched out in a 15-mile line in the path of the advance...

Communist-led troops cut Highway 1, the capital's overloaded highway to the coast, and Highway 4, its lifeline to the food producing Mekong Delta to the south.

The Morning Herald, Uniontown, Pennsylvania, Monday, April 28, 1975

Benjamin Stoddert loitered in the Vung Tau holding area for the second week of April and then, surprisingly, we were ordered back to Subic Bay, arriving on the 17th. In fact, almost all of the principal ships of the U.S. Seventh Fleet which would soon be actively engaged in the evacuation of South Vietnam were either waiting in port or, like

Stoddert, being sent into ports across the theater. Here is a list of those ships and where they were on the morning of Friday, April 18:

At Subic Bay

USS Midway (CVA-41)
USS Okinawa (LPH-3)
USS Vancouver (LPD-2)
USS Thomaston (LAD-2)
USS Peoria (LST-1183)
USS Blue Ridge (LCC-19) – Flagship for Commander Task Force 76
USS Dubuque (LPD-8)
USS Benjamin Stoddert (DDG-22)
USS Knox (DE-1052)
USS Cochrane (DDG-21)
USS Henry P. Wilson (DDG-7)
USS Worden (DLG-18)
USS Rowan (DD-782)
USS Gurke (DD-783)
USS John Paul Jones (DDG-32)

At Manila

USS Enterprise (CVAN-65)
USS Reasoner (DE-1063)

At Singapore

USS Handcock (CVA-19)
USS Kirk (DE-1083)
USS Cook (DE-1087)

In Hong Kong

USS Durham (LKA-114)
USS Frederick (LST-1184)

At Okinawa

USS Denver (LPD-9)
USS Duluth (LPD-6)
USS Mobile (LKA-113)
USS Mount Vernon (LSD-39)
USS Tuscaloosa (LST-1187)
USS Barbour County (LST-195)

At Iwakuni, Japan

USS Anchorage (LSD-36)

And at Sea

USS Oklahoma City (CLG-5) – Flagship for Commander, Seventh Fleet
USS Coral Sea (CVA-43) – Flagship for Commander Task Force 77
USS Gridley (DLG-21)
USS Meyerkord (DE-1058)
USS Bausell (DD-845)

(Note: Any of these ships with designations beginning with an "L" were the various configurations of amphibious ships; those with "D" were destroyers or destroyer escorts (known as, and soon to be officially re-designated as frigates; those with "CV" were strike aircraft carriers; and those with "CL" were light cruisers.)

On the morning of the April 17, just before entering Subic Bay, we conducted an underway replenishment to receive fuel from the fleet oiler *USNS Passumpsic (T-AO-107).* (Most Navy supply ships had Native American tribe names.) Then, just before 1500 that afternoon, we moored at the Riviera Pier (the destroyer pier) furthest outboard in a nest of four ships docked side-by-side. It was a rare and impressive sight to see four beautiful *Charles F. Adams-class* DDG's tied up together: *Stoddert* with our sister ship *Cochran,* along with *John Paul Jones,* and *Henry B. Wilson.*

That evening, my crewmates and I, except those unlucky few in the duty section, were granted on-base-only liberty. That meant an opportunity to call Sharon and also to head over to the Chuck Wagon Club for what might be my last slices of pizza and Subic Specials for who knows how long. We expected, as did the crews of those other three ships tied up with us, that a return to Vung Tau or somewhere near Vietnam was just as inevitable as the fall of Saigon. I was extremely lucky to have left the ship at 1545 with orders to be back by 2000, because at 1600 no one else was allowed to go on liberty and the ship was on a four hour standby to get underway. I sauntered back on board at about 1800 and I could tell from the pace of activity that we were on a very short fuse.

By mid-morning the next day, April 18, Subic Bay was in chaos as ships were headed out to sea, and all of those ports listed above were being quickly emptied as well. Clearly, it was "go time." *Stoddert* was again underway, this time escorting *USS Dubuque (LPD-8),* an *Austin*-class amphibious transport dock. LPD's were one of the larger classes of the American amphibious ship fleet, measuring about 570 feet in length and, in addition to having the capability of launching and retrieving landing craft at its aft-end flooded dock, it had a large enough flight deck to simultaneously operate two large helicopters, such as the twin-rotor CH-46 or the CH-53, or four small UH-1 (Huey) copters. In the two weeks that followed, we spent *a lot* of time with the *Dubuque.* Our deck log entry for one minute after midnight that night was, *"In transit from Subic Bay to Vung Tau. Operating with USS Dubuque. OTC* (officer in tactical command) *and SOPA* (senior officer present afloat) *are CTG* (Commander Task Group) *76.5. Flagship is USS Dubuque."* We arrived off Vung Tau at noon the following day, which was Sunday, April 20. The Republic of Viet Nam had only ten days left in existence.

In the introduction to this book I mentioned the 2014 feature-length documentary by Rory Kennedy, the youngest of the eleven children of the assassinated presidential candidate and U.S. Senator Robert F. "Bobby" Kennedy. Her film "The Last Days of Vietnam" does an excellent job describing the emotional story of the final days leading up to the eventual evacuation of Saigon by helicopter on April 29-30, officially called Operation Frequent Wind. With the searing imagery of actual film footage shot in and around Saigon and current day interviews with several of the principal individuals involved at the time, Ms. Kennedy's film conveys a tremendous amount of information and a visceral sense of the danger and emotions of those days.

There are a couple of excellent books on the end of the war, listed in my "recommended reading" at the end of this book. Also available on the internet is the 199-page report enigmatically titled "NEMVAC SURVEY REPORT 4-19 MAY 1975." Immediately after the completion of Operation Frequent Wind, the Chairman of the Joint Chiefs of Staff (CJCS), Air Force General George S. Brown, dispatched a team of staff officers led by Army Major General John R. D. Cleland, Jr. to interview commanders and their staffs of all of the major elements in the operation. The cover sheet of this report was hand-labeled "Excised Version, 25 Aug 80," which probably indicates the date on which the report was declassified. The document appears almost complete in its content with very few places where text was removed due to its continued sensitivity and/or classification. Each page has its original classification markings at the top and bottom of the page blacked out... except for three pages where the censor failed, no doubt a simple oversight, to black out the word "SECRET," the original security classification of the entire report. And I also suspect there was almost certainly a TOP SECRET addendum to the report, all references to which were no doubt among those few areas which were redacted (removed) from the document now available to the public. Not surprisingly, I couldn't find a declassified copy of any such addendum.

NEMVAC is the military abbreviation for "Non-combatant Emergency & Evacuation Plan." The document is replete with additional acronyms, the glossary for which goes on for three pages and includes seventy-three items. And those were only the acronyms arcane enough, in the opinion of the report preparers, to warrant explanations. This is typical of military reports as they're really intended only for military readers.

The first paragraph of the executive summary provides the reason for the report. The author says, "The specific purpose of the evaluation was to insure the best possible readiness of US Forces to conduct NEMVAC operations under all conditions worldwide, should circumstances again require such operations." Clearly, good planning – as had been done well in advance for Frequent Wind – helps achieve a successful mission, which, while it wasn't pretty, the evacuation of Saigon achieved. And equally clearly, a post-mission "task of validating important lessons learned from the recent emergency evacuation of South Vietnam" was the goal. There were indeed a lot of lessons to be learned.

The report is comprehensive and pretty interesting, written in the typical military style with a short and readable executive summary followed by a confusing bird's nest of numbered and lettered annexes, appendices, and tabs. But overall, it provides a thorough description of these elements: the planning process, which had been begun a full year earlier in anticipation of the fall of Saigon; the command and organizational structure of forces from all of the participating branches of the armed forces; and the chronology of events, complete with the number of aircraft sorties from each launching platform and each evacuation landing zone. It provides a detailed report on the telecommunications network plans and lists all key messages among the principal players as the operation unfolded. Most interesting is the report's direct but diplomatic description of the difficult, but thankfully not disabling, undercurrent of confusion and misunderstandings created by the awkward division of operational responsibility between the multiple levels of the military commander structure on the ground in Vietnam, offshore, at Pearl Harbor and Washington, and Ambassador Martin at the embassy in Saigon.

Drawing from the Kennedy documentary, this NEMVAC report, and other sources, here's the essence of how things happened in the final days of the war, leading to the evacuation of all Americans who chose to leave and many thousands of South Vietnamese. Our ship played a supportive role, providing our guns and missiles as elements of a protective shield which also included tactical fighter aircraft from the carriers for the evacuation ships in the days leading up to the fateful date of April 29.

Four options for the evacuation of South Vietnam had been planned in advance:

Option I: Evacuation by commercial aircraft from Tan Son Nhut and other airports in South Vietnam.

Option II: Evacuation by military aircraft from Tan Son Nhut and other airports.

Option III: Evacuation by sea lift from Saigon port.

Option IV: Evacuation by helicopters to U.S. Navy ships offshore, primarily from the Defense Attaché Office (DAO) compound, with only embassy and security force personnel evacuation from the embassy compound itself.

Operation Frequent Wind, the helicopter-borne evacuation, was the fourth and least attractive of four options that had been evaluated and planned for extracting the thousands of Americans and tens of thousands of Vietnamese nationals who would be in danger due to their close collaboration with Americans during the war. However, planning for that option never anticipated that the U.S. Embassy in downtown Saigon would become a primary extraction site for a large scale air lift by helicopters. Planning documents anticipated only about a hundred embassy personnel would evacuate directly from the embassy. The DAO, which was adjacent to Tan Son Nhut airport, was ideal for a large scale evacuation and featured prominently in all four options because of the favorable layout and security for landing zones. Any evacuation from the DAO would have to be completed well before that location became too vulnerable to attacks by the approaching North Vietnamese army.

A wholesale evacuation was going to be a very large and complex operation, and timing was essential. A similar and more modest plan, by the way, for the evacuation of Phnom Penh, Cambodia had already been successfully accomplished on April 12 under the code name Operation Eagle Pull, five days before Cambodia collapsed.

Beginning in late March, hundreds of people were able to leave Vietnam by both commercial and military aircraft, even though no formal evacuation had yet been ordered. As stated earlier, Ambassador Martin, who was charged with the responsibility of actually making evacuation decisions, refused to take any official action, still believing the protection of Saigon and the surrounding region could be maintained. And also, no doubt, the Ambassador knew any outward signs that the Americans were evacuating would set off panic among the Vietnamese who were working with them, and among the public in general.

In late March and early April, commercial planes and Military Airlift Command (MAC) chartered aircraft were arriving and departing from Tan Son Nhut, many of them evacuating civilians and Vietnamese orphans. Unfortunately, the tragic crash of the Air Force C-5A had resulted in the grounding of the entire fleet of those huge military transport planes, leaving the Air Force with only much smaller C-141 and C-130 aircraft. Later in April, as conditions at the airport became more dangerous, even the C-141's, which required a longer runway and were less maneuverable, were taken out of this service, leaving only the C-130's. Those Lockheed-built turbo-prop aircraft were nominally authorized for only 75 passengers, although those restrictions were increasingly ignored as more and more fearful Vietnamese were being packed onto each flight out. While Vietnamese aircraft were being commandeered by RVN military pilots and flown to Thailand and other destinations in the region, most American military flights were going to Clark Air Force base near Manila. However, due to restrictions imposed on the number of refugees allowed into his country by Philippine President Ferdinand Marcos, over-pressed MAC aircraft had to carry refugees onward to various destinations, including Guam, Wake Island, Yokota, Japan, and even all the way to Hawaii.

Even though not officially ordered, Options I and II were being executed in a *de facto* fashion and, according to some sources, these actions were essentially being done behind the back of the Ambassador. The Kennedy documentary contains interviews with some of the Defense and State Departments' officials who had decided to take matters into their own hands and start the fixed wing evacuations without any formal authority. Americans who were trying to get Vietnamese family members or close associates out were also being hampered by South Vietnamese bureaucratic delays in clearing their paperwork, but eventually, paperwork was pretty much ignored as the clamoring to get out became more urgent.

Option III, a boat lift, was also never officially ordered. But with that said, in the last week of April, pretty much any ships floating in the Saigon River were also being loaded with people and put out to sea. There's a harrowing story of American Consul-General Terry McNamara organizing a flotilla at Can Tho to evacuate his people down the Bassac River in the Mekong Delta. No sooner had they gotten underway, they were ordered by an RVN Navy patrol boat to heave-to to be searched for deserters. Since McNamara had among his evacuees some Vietnamese who had served as intelligence agents, he feared the worst. Fortunately, however, he knew the RVN commander on the scene and had actually helped that officer's family to evacuate a short time earlier, so the flotilla was allowed to proceed. Before reaching the sea, he transferred all Americans and the highest value Vietnamese from other boats to his own landing craft and increased his speed downriver. Shortly after that transfer, his boat came under fire from the river bank, and the small team of Marines he had with him returned fire with grenade launchers and automatic rifles. This brief action became known as the "last American combat action of the war," according to a report filed by Staff Sergeant Boyette S. Hasty. He reported: "1500 on the afternoon of 29 April. Last shots fired against the enemy." McNamara and his people made it to the South China Sea thanks to one additional bit of good fortune – a very heavy rainfall that arrived just in time to cloak their passage through the dangerous narrows at the mouth of the river where they expected to be most vulnerable.

A waterborne evacuation was also happening at Saigon. Tugs,

barges, and the former American landing ship LST-117, manned by a Korean crew and renamed *Boo Hueng Pioneer,* took on a large number of people and departed the Newport docks just upstream of Saigon at about noon on April 29. There was chaos in the narrow channel with groundings, collisions, and general confusion, but eventually the flotilla approached the Khanh Hoi docks near downtown, finding the wharf teeming with more people desperate to board any ship heading down river. A tug with two barges arrived mid-afternoon, and about 6,000 people were able to be embarked, including those who had arrived on bus convoys arranged by embassy staff members. By the time the final barges pushed off just before 1730, it seemed as though everyone who wanted to leave the docks had embarked and there was still room on board for more. In spite of the risks of getting the flotilla downriver, and the chaos of passing through the narrow channel again, all of the boats eventually made it to international waters during the night.

And then, of course, was the famous helicopter-borne evacuation of Saigon. From all over the city and the immediately surrounding area, American civilians and military personnel, friendly foreigners, and international diplomats who had for one reason or another failed to be extracted by their own countries' evacuation efforts in the preceding weeks, were being brought to the DAO compound by pre-positioned buses. They had been told to tune in to the Saigon commercial radio station and listen for the code words "it's 112 degrees and rising," followed by the surrealistic playing of Irving Berlin's "White Christmas." When they heard it, they were to proceed quickly to the bus pickup, which had happened during the morning of the 29th. Soon there was a large number of people at the compound ready and anxious to get out.

Going back to 1110 Saigon time on the previous day, the 28th, the Commander in Chief, Pacific (CINCPAC) had placed all Frequent Wind forces on a one hour alert status, then briefly changed this order to a six hour alert, and then, just as quickly, back to one hour alert due to reports coming in as to the worsening military situation around the city. At 2212 that evening, CINCPAC ordered military forces to plan for an all-out evacuation by C-130 aircraft from Tan Son Nhut, beginning at first light on the 29th, with a plan to evacuate about 9,000 people per day. Execution would be on the order of CINCPAC himself.

At 0209 on April 29, that order was given. Airborne tankers and the Airborne Battlefield Command and Control Center EC-130 aircraft were launched and arrived on station during the night to support the C-130 evacuation operations from Tan Son Nhut in the morning. But those fixed wing operations never even got started since rockets, infantry gun shells, and bombs had begun falling on the airport.

As the morning of April 29 dawned, the Ambassador still expected the C-130 evacuation to begin. But when he was advised by the on-site commander at Tan Son Nhut that the airport was taking fire, and conducting flight operations by airplanes would no longer be safe, Ambassador Martin did what, in retrospect, was either heroically brave or incredibly stupid. He asked to be immediately driven to the airport to assess the situation himself. Not surprisingly, he quickly confirmed what the military commander had told him by phone and hastily returned to the embassy. The Ambassador, CINCPAC, and the Chairman of the Joint Chiefs of Staff (CJCS) quickly conferred by secure communications and decided that since Tan Son Nhut airport was no longer suitable for fixed wing aircraft operations, with the hesitant agreement from the Ambassador, authority was needed from the White House to execute Operation Frequent Wind – the helicopter evacuation of U.S. citizens and designated Vietnamese from the DAO compound and the embassy. With authority quickly granted by the President, the CJCS formally ordered execution of that option at 1050 Saigon time on Tuesday, April 29. The end was irrevocably beginning.

The first three Marine Corps CH-53 helicopters lifted off from Task Force 76 ships and landed at the DAO compound at 1506, inserting 105 ground support force troops, and lifted off less than ten minutes later with the first group of evacuees. Although many hundreds of people, perhaps even thousands, had escaped from the city in the preceding days and weeks through the unofficial evacuation efforts, these 149 people were the first official evacuees of Frequent Wind. Throughout the afternoon, more defensive troops were brought into the compound, and a smooth and orderly evacuation proceeded using four landing zones that had been marked with fluorescent paint to facilitate landings. The helicopters did receive periodic small arms ground fire, but there were no casualties. The operation was textbook: well-planned and professionally executed.

At the embassy compound, however, a crisis situation was quickly developing. Desperate Vietnamese were pushing their way through the gates and climbing over the walls by the hundreds in spite of the efforts of the Marine guards to stop them. Some had papers indicating American employment or status and others had friends among the Americans at the embassy. And some were just too persistent to be kept out. By 1500, the approximately 100 expected evacuees from that location had become more than 2,000. As stated earlier, plans for Frequent Wind had never included considerations of such numbers, but there was no way for them to be turned away and sent to the DAO compound. The decision was quickly made by the Ambassador and military commanders to immediately expand helicopter operations at the embassy, employing twin rotor CH-46's for evacuation. A large tree in the parking area near the entrance to the main building, which had for years been a source of beauty and pride for the Ambassador and his staff, was cut down and paint was used to mark a landing zone. At 1735, the first four Marine Corps CH-46's lifted off from ships offshore and landed at the embassy at 1800, simultaneous with the third wave of H-53's in the cyclic operations at the DAO compound.

By just before 1900, the Ambassador notified the Task Force Commander that he had 2,500 people still needing evacuation at the embassy and so flight operations into and out of both sites continued past sunset, just as a new challenge presented itself – the weather. Throughout the afternoon the low clouds and intermittent rain, common for Vietnam, had worsened, and, with the coming of darkness, the American pilots also had to contend with very low ceilings and periods of heavy rain, making the flying more difficult. At the same time, they were increasingly exhausted from hours of flying and harrowing landings both in the tight landing zones ashore and on moving ships at sea. Aboard the flagship, *USS Blue Ridge,* there was talk at one point of suspending flights into the embassy until morning, but Marine Brigadier General Richard A. Carey, assistant commander of the First Marine Air Wing and the on-scene commander of the USMC flight operations, would hear none of it. The pilots were Marines, he said, and they'd get the job done. While operations at the DAO compound were essentially over, ending with the extraction of the ground support force, there were many people at the embassy and, he pointed out, there might not be any chances of resuming flights in the morning with the Communists overrunning the city. And so the flights continued into the night.

During the day on the 29th, there were plenty more helicopters in the air than the H-53's and CH-46's of the Frequent Wind forces. Air America, the quasi-private company operated by the CIA, was also doing what it could in helping Americans and Vietnamese nationals to escape using two dozen of its UH-1 (Huey) birds operated by 31 volunteer pilots. Normally, a Huey had a two man flight crew, but for this emergency, most of the copters were flown by a single pilot in order to load as many evacuees as possible on each flight, often exceeding what would normally be a safe number of passengers for that type of aircraft. Pickups were being made from rooftop landing zones around the city, and passengers were either dropped off at the DAO compound for onward extraction by the Marine pilots or flown out to the Task Force 76 ships offshore.

One of the Air America missions was famously captured by a Saigon-based United Press International (UPI) photographer named Hubert van Es. His picture of a UH-1 on a rooftop picking up evacuees became the quintessential symbol of the evacuation of Saigon and stylized as the logo of the Broadway show "Miss Saigon." In current day popular culture, many people believe this picture was "the last helicopter on the last day" from the U.S. Embassy. But it was actually taken during the daylight hours of the 29th at the Pittman apartment building at 22 Gia Long Street, which was used as living quarters for various employees of the embassy, CIA, and USAID.

With the beleaguered throngs trying to leave the city, the official airborne evacuation was winding to an intense and exhausting close. At 1930 at the DAO compound, General Carey ordered the transfer by air of the Marine security force at the compound, about 130 in number, over to the embassy to augment physical security for the evacuation. The last evacuees at the DAO compound were loaded onto helicopters at 2030 and flown out, followed by the withdrawal of the last of the security force at that location, lifting off at about 2230, just as thermite bombs they had placed in strategic locations destroyed the communications infrastructure and sensitive documents. The DAO evacuation – the one that had actually been planned for – was successfully completed.

At the embassy, however, the situation remained critical. Exhausted Marine Corps air crews were still making shuttle runs in terrible weather from the fleet to the parking lot landing zone as the evening became the dead of night. By 0215 in the morning on the 30th, two helicopters were landing about every ten minutes. There were multiple recounts of the Americans and non-Americans still waiting to leave and, at that time, there were still about a thousand people in all. All of them were being told over and over again that "nobody would be left behind." About this time, the embassy told Admiral Whitmire that they estimated another 19 lifts would complete the evacuation – that number clearly not jibing with the number of people waiting. But that number was relayed all the way to the anxious White House, and the order came back directly from President Ford that no more than that number would be allowed.

To punctuate these orders, the overhead flying command post began to broadcast this message over radios to all of the helicopters:

The following message is from the President of the United States and should be passed on by the first helicopter in contact with Ambassador Martin. Only 21 lifts remain. Americans only will be transported. Ambassador Martin will board the first available helicopter and that helicopter will broadcast "Tiger, Tiger, Tiger" once it is airborne and en route.

At 0430 on the 30th, however, operations were continuing, and both the 19 and 21 flight limits had been passed, still carrying both American and Vietnamese people in spite of the content of that presidential order. And hundreds of people, including Ambassador Martin, were still at the embassy. A final count was made of the people waiting – all of whom had been promised multiple times they would not be left behind. It was quickly estimated that all of them could be lifted out with six more aircraft. At this point, however, the on-the-scene Marine commander, Major James Kean, spoke with General Carey over one of the helicopter radios and was given the no-kidding directive that from that point on, the airlift would truly only evacuate Americans. Kean was further ordered to withdraw these American-only evacuees and his security forces into the Chancery building and retreat to the rooftop landing zone for evacuation. We have that iconic picture of a Huey loading people from the rooftop of the residence in downtown Saigon, but there just aren't any pictures of these last flights from the embassy.

Reluctantly, but under direct orders from the President, Ambassador Martin boarded a CH-46, which lifted off outbound to the *USS Blue Ridge* at 0458 on April 30, with the pilot radioing "Tiger, Tiger, Tiger." All that remained on that rooftop, with the elevators disabled and doors to the roof barricaded and guarded, were Major Kean and his Marines of the security force. These men had to wait for what seemed like ages – about two hours – for the helicopters to return for their extraction. Meanwhile gunfire was popping from nearby buildings as snipers were trying to hit the Marines. The dawn came, and as the sun was rising into what was just another hot, humid Saigon day, the helicopters returned to pick them up. It took nine birds to take them all. Finally, there were only Major Kean and ten enlisted Marines. The last CH-46 finally touched down and took these men aboard with Master Gunnery Sergeant Juan Valdez the last man to board. They lifted off at 0753 and flew out to the *USS Okinawa,* landing at 0830, marking the official end of Operation Frequent Wind. Sadly, however, there were still over four hundred bewildered Vietnamese who had been abandoned at the embassy – along with all of America's hopes for something other than an ignominious defeat in Vietnam. But one can't compare the actual misery and, for many, death, that followed for those people left behind with the loss of American prestige. For America, it was a grave disappointment. For the doomed, it was utter tragedy.

And then, of course, there were the many small airplanes and various helicopters belonging to the Republic of Vietnam government forces. Piloted by Vietnamese military pilots, they were flying all over the area picking up family members or colleagues and then either heading in the direction of Thailand or out to sea to find any Navy deck they could to land on. Many of these pilots made multiple round trips in heroic efforts to help as many of their countrymen and women as possible. There are tales of harrowing landings on tightly packed flight decks or of hovering and lowering passengers to the ships. One story is that of a Huey pilot lowering his passengers to the deck of a ship and ditching the aircraft in the sea nearby, with the brave pilot literally jumping out of the bird as it settled on the surface, broke apart, and sank. The pilot then swam to the ship and was pulled aboard.

That ditching incident happened with the *USS Kirk (DE-1087)*, a *Knox*-class destroyer escort. It was only one of the stories associated with that ship which became legendary for its actions off the coast of Vietnam. Its flight deck, designed for the operation of its single antisubmarine SH-2 Seasprite helicopter, quickly became a landing target for Hueys flying out from shore. Commander Paul Jacobs, her commanding officer, ordered their own ship's aircraft to be stowed in their small hangar which cleared his deck to receive multiple landings. After a Huey landed and unloaded, the ship's crew literally pushed it over the side to make room for the next bird coming in, something they did several times. In a final and stunning act of bravery, with her flight deck and her aft fantail area each holding a Huey that they planned to bring back for salvage, her own SH-2 pilot was lifted by a cable to a hovering Huey which had no place to land with the flight deck occupied, and took over the controls, allowing the Vietnamese pilot to be lowered to the deck. The Navy pilot, now alone in the aircraft, ascended and then made an extremely perilous landing forward of the ship's gun mount on the focs'le. Apparently, the ship's crew had determined the exact dimensions of the Huey's rotors and of the distance from the single flat area on the bow to their forward gun mount and calculated the helicopter could be landed there with about a foot of clearance. That they actually carried out this landing was stunning, and probably foolish since they were risking the safety of the ship and the crew just to save a used Huey. But they did it anyway. I got goose bumps when we on the *Stoddert* actually saw *Kirk* just outside Subic Bay several days later, and counted three Hueys on deck. We were utterly amazed at the feat they had accomplished.

In describing the actions of the *Kirk,* I should mention my own very minor connection to that ship. Nine months before these events, I had the good fortune to spend three days underway aboard *Kirk* off the coast of San Diego, as part of my six-week antisubmarine warfare officer's school. I had been assigned to attend that training course before Sharon and I flew out to Hawaii for me to join the *Benjamin Stoddert* crew. The *USS Kirk* had a tremendous reputation for excellence, and it was a pleasure to watch her officers and crew in action while I got a reminder of what life at sea was like over those three memorable days on a small but very capable ship.

While the airborne evacuation of South Vietnam was underway, either officially as part of Frequent Wind or otherwise, boats of all sizes were putting off from shore with thousands upon thousands of people desperate to leave. Task Force 76 ships and merchant ships from several countries anchored or cruising just offshore were taking droves of people aboard from fishing boats and other small craft. But what about the RVN Navy's ships?

The *USS Kirk* was to play a prominent role in what was to happen with the RVN ships that had managed to get to sea. There were no longer any home country ports for them to return to, and many of their crews had taken aboard their families or others trying to get out. These friends and allies of the United States needed help, and Rear Admiral Whitmire, the Task Force Commander, hastily put together a plan that would be overseen by a civilian based on a U.S. Navy ship – the *Kirk.* That man was a U.S. Naval Academy Class of

'67 graduate named Richard (Dick) Armitage. He had been a Navy intelligence officer serving with distinction in South Vietnam before transferring back to Washington as a civilian in the intelligence community.

During the years of his Vietnam service, Mr. Armitage had made many friends in their military and was someone they could trust. With the collapse of the country nearing, the Pentagon sent him back to Vietnam to oversee the important mission of protecting sensitive naval technology by either removing or destroying ships of the RVN fleet from the country to keep them out of the hands of the Communists. On April 30, the Admiral sent orders to Captain Jacobs on the *Kirk* to embark Mr. Armitage and follow orders from him. While every person in the American military knows they serve under a civilian leadership in Washington, the commanding officer of a Navy ship is certainly not accustomed to having a civilian issuing orders on his ship. In Rory Kennedy's documentary film, Captain Jacobs spoke about how he and Mr. Armitage quickly took stock of each other and realized they would make a great team. And indeed they did.

On April 30, *Kirk* set out for Dao Con Son, an island just over 45 nautical miles from the coast which had not yet fallen to the North Vietnamese and was the former site of an infamous prison. Gathering in its harbors were the remnants of the RVN Navy that were still afloat and had crews to man them. Together, Mr. Armitage and Captain Jacobs gathered that little fleet, with *Kirk* as its flagship, and on May 2 set off in a convoy toward Subic Bay.

In order to ease the question of diplomatic issues with the Philippine government, just before their arrival in Subic, the flotilla stopped and held a solemn at-sea decommissioning ceremony with as much pomp and circumstance as the grim situation allowed. To saluting ranks of sailors on each ship, the national flag of the Republic of Vietnam was hauled down and the Stars and Stripes of the United States were hoisted on the now American-owned ships. It had been no small feat to find enough American flags among *Kirk's* spares and other ships that had joined company.

Commander Paul Jacobs was celebrated as a hero in the U.S. Navy and ultimately retired with the rank of captain. I heard him speak in late 2014 at a Washington, DC screening of the Kennedy documentary film. There was still a gleam in his eyes, conveying his quiet pride for the role he and his crew had in those final days. And Dick Armitage resumed his career in the U.S. intelligence and diplomatic services, ultimately serving as the second in command of the State Department under the leadership of Secretary Colin Powell in President George W. Bush's Administration.

Over the final two days, the Marines had flown 1,054 flight hours on 682 sorties throughout the operation. Three hundred and ninety-five Americans and 4,475 Vietnamese and third-country nationals were lifted from the DAO compound, and 978 Americans and 1,120 Vietnamese and third-country nationals had been flown out of the embassy. There were only four casualties of the whole operation: two Marine corporals, Charles McMahon and Darwin Judge, were killed at the DAO compound, and two Marine pilots of a CH-46 from the *USS Hancock.* Those pilots, Captain William Nystul and First Lieutenant Michael Shea, were lost when their aircraft crashed approaching the ship. That copter's two enlisted crewmen were rescued, but the bodies of the pilots were never recovered. It was those four Marines whose names are on the wall at the Vietnam Veterans Memorial in Washington as the last fatalities of U.S. armed forces to die in the Vietnam War. The two crew members of an AH-1J Sea Cobra that was ditched at sea after running out of fuel were safely recovered (by the mighty ship *Kirk*) and an A-7 Corsair from the *USS Midway* suffered an engine failure while providing overhead air cover for the helicopter operations, causing the pilot to eject. He too was rescued unhurt.

In the two weeks that followed the end of the Vietnam War, the Cambodian Khmer Rouge brazenly seized the American merchant ship *SS Mayaguez* in international waters and, unfortunately, several more service members died in the fierce battle to recover the ship and its crew. Fittingly, their names too are on "the wall." But this happened in Cambodian waters and not Vietnam. By the morning of April 30, all American forces had left the ground of Vietnam and the ships of Task Force 76 were withdrawing out to international waters and setting off to various destinations, but that page of history regarding *the last Americans to leave* was still to be written by the *Benjamin Stoddert* and those serving on her crew.

CHAPTER 18

Secret Mission

WASHINGTON (AP) – President Ford spent an anxious 24 hours as he made the decision for an all-out evacuation of Americans from Saigon and waited for the last helicopter to leave safely.

When it was all over late Tuesday afternoon and he closed "a chapter in the American experience," Ford asked the nation "to close ranks ... avoid recriminations... to work together on the great tasks that remain to be accomplished."

Cumberland Evening Times, Cumberland, Maryland,
Wednesday, April 30, 1975

As the evacuation was taking place on April 29, the *Benjamin Stoddert*, operating offshore, was listening to what was happening. A special watch had been set up in CIC for a team of men to listen to and write down the voice transmissions made by the Marines at the embassy, and to the best of our ability make sure they were being relayed to the Task Force Commander – sometimes by us. This gave several of our crewmembers the sense of "being there" with the Marines in their hellish circumstances, yet totally helpless to save them, right up to the end. Over the radio, our guys could hear the gunshots being fired to defend the Marines' perch on the rooftop secured until the last men were evacuated. John Brandl, my friend and roommate for most of the cruise, was one of the guys standing these watches and recently told me he had suffered from disturbing nightmares for a long time after our safe return.

And yet, while all this was happening ashore on April 29, *Stoddert* received new and highly classified orders for a different mission, one which would take us away from the Vung Tau operating area, even though our team in CIC was still able to monitor the radio transmissions from the Embassy. A sounding of our fuel tanks at noon that day showed we were at 69.5% capacity on fuel oil for our boilers and 73% for the diesel fuel for our two ship's boats. For the mission we were assigned, we needed to top off our fuel tanks, and so in the early afternoon we pulled up to the starboard side of a fleet oiler, the *USS Kiwishiwi (AO-146),* to refuel with Lieutenant Dave LaValley controlling the ship as the conning officer.

Unfortunately, though, we weren't able to completely fill our tanks. Midway through the fueling, an alarm sounded, indicating a possible failure of the gyrocompass, a critically required system when maneuvering at fifteen knots alongside another ship that's only fifty feet away. The captain immediately took the conn and ordered an emergency breakaway. Not having an assigned station for the refueling detail, I was standing at the back of the bridge watching the underway replenishment as part of my self-assigned training. What I observed was a textbook job of maintaining control of the ship, ever so slightly edging away from *Kiwishiwi* while the fore and aft fuel lines were disconnected and sent back to the oiler, and then the rest of the connecting wire ropes from which the hoses had been suspended were sent back and all lines then cast off. As soon as all lines were clear, the captain ordered "all ahead flank" and we turned sharply to starboard as soon as we had pulled ahead. Although the fuse that had blown in the compass was quickly replaced, bringing it back online, we weren't able to get a second chance to finish refueling. We had to depart the area quickly to catch and rejoin the *USS Dubuque.*

Dubuque had left the evacuation fleet's operating area just after dark the previous evening to sail around the southern tip of South Vietnam and then go up the country's western coast toward an island called Dao Phu Quoc. Also under highly classified orders, she was to position herself near the island to provide a navigational beacon and possible refueling station for South Vietnamese aircraft fleeing not to the Philippines, but to Thailand. We were to bring our firepower and join her there. After that emergency breakaway from the *Kiwishiwi*, we set a course of 240 degrees and speed 20 knots, which is about the maximum speed we could go on a fuel-efficient run with only two of our four boilers on the line. And it's a good thing we hadn't lit off a third boiler, because that was the last fuel we were to get for a long time.

To help document this story, I've been able to recreate the timeline of events on our ship from the copy of our deck logs I had obtained from the National Archives. But the next part of the story must come from my memory and conversations with fellow officers, as several days' pages from the logs I received for this particular period were redacted. This was probably because they had never been declassified from a higher classification level – almost certainly "Top Secret." The last log entries I could see for the night of April 29-30 were these:

2229: SIGHTED HON KHOAI NAV LIGHT – BEARING 287 T

Hon Khoi is a very small island just off the southernmost tip of South Vietnam. Our course was set to pass it to seaward on our starboard side.

> 0000: ASSUMED THE WATCH UNDERWAY IN ACCORDANCE WITH SEVENTHFLT QUARTERLY EMPLOYMENT SCHEDULE. OPERATING WITH USS DUBUQUE. SOPA IS CTF 76. FLAGSHIP IS USS BLUE RIDGE. BOILERS ON THE LINE ARE 1B & 2B. GENERATORS ON THE LINE ARE 1A+1B+2B. THE PLANT IS SPLIT. THE SHIP IS DARKENED. MATERIAL CONDITION YOKE IS SET THROUGHOUT THE SHIP. CONDITION OF READINESS III.

This indicates we were officially operating with *Dubuque,* even though we had not yet caught up with her, and we were still under the operating authority of Rear Admiral Whitmire, Commander Task Force 76 embarked on the *Blue Ridge,* which had not yet left Vung Tau. It shows we were indeed steaming on two boilers with three electrical generators on the line with one engine receiving steam from one boiler and the other engine from the other boiler. Condition Yoke and Readiness level III constituted our standard non-combat readiness posture regarding watertight hatches being closed and weapon systems manning. And the ship's exterior lighting was the standard condition with only our masthead, side, and stern running lights visible.

Beyond these entries, my declassified copy of our ship's log showed no more entries until Sunday, May 11. The fact that those log pages were missing for the next ten days is part of what makes what follows intriguing. We were on what could rightfully be called a top secret mission. Our passage that next day was a scene right out of the haunting Francis Ford Coppola movie, *Apocalypse Now.* The captain and some of the more senior officers knew what was up, but most of the crew, including me, were kept in the dark.

Just after dawn on April 30, having rounded Hon Khoai and heading northward along the coast toward Dao Phu Quok Island, we passed a merchant cargo ship at anchor close to shore. From a distance, the rusted vessel looked like a piece of rotted fruit crawling with ants, because her decks were covered with literally thousands of people, and even more who had come out from shore in small boats were trying to climb up an accommodation ladder rigged over her side. She was trying to rescue as many people as possible, but we didn't know anything about whose authority she was doing this under or even who owner her. Her Master called to us by radio with a plea for help, saying something like: "American Navy ship 22 passing: Please stay and provide gun cover for me as I load passengers." Quickly assessing the situation, Captain Hekman didn't hesitate for a moment. He had no authorization to divert from our mission or to use any kind of force other than in very clear self-defense. And so his reply, spoken emphatically over the radio to the merchant went something like this: "Captain, I recommend you get the hell out of here. You need to slip (cut loose) your anchor and leave… right now!" And then we watched in fascination as the merchant's anchor chain went overboard and they cut away the ladder with people still trying to climb up. It was unfathomable were I not there to see it with my own eyes.

A couple of hours later, we rejoined *Dubuque* off of Phu Quoc. In addition to her stated mission of providing a navigation beacon and possible on-deck refueling for South Vietnamese aircraft fleeing to Thailand, her crew was also supporting the merchant ships under contract with the American Military Sealift Command (MSC) loading refugees there. We stood off to seaward and played no role in any of this, but for the *Dubuque's* crew, this probably seemed like a return to hell. She had been to the island before.

As the month of March had ended, Republic of Vietnam cities to the north of Saigon were falling fast – in most cases not as a result of Communist forces but rather at the hands of renegade RVN troops who, having been deserted by their officers, began looting and fighting among themselves. This naturally sent a tremendous wave of the population fleeing their homes for the relative safety of Saigon to the south. The RVN government, in collaboration with the American MSC, had hired ships to load refugees at ports such as Da Nang, Cam Rahn Bay, and Phan Rang. Among the ships were the civilian-crewed Navy cargo ships *USNS Greenville Victory* and *USNS Sgt. Andrew Miller,* plus the commercial sister ships *SS Pioneer Challenger* and *Pioneer Contender.* All had been grossly overloaded with refugees and ordered to take their human cargoes to Phu Quoc Island, the site of a former prisoner of war camp, where the RVN government had provided assurances that they would find food, water, and safe shelter. But these civilian ships were badly understaffed and unprepared to feed a huge number of people, maintain security, or even provide for basic sanitation. And then they discovered the conditions at Phu Quoc were just as bad, since the promised food and services were simply not in place there.

The most harrowing of the tales coming from this early-April operation concerned the 455 foot long *Geenville Victory* under the command of Captain Raymond Iaobacci. They had taken aboard what may have been as many as ten thousand people at Cam Rahn Bay, many of them armed RVN soldiers fleeing Da Nang. With this mass of humanity basically starving and exposed on deck, there was a near riot on board as the ship sailed past Vung Tau and continued southwest and then around the coast to Phu Quoc. As she anchored at the island on April 4, an RVN patrol boat came near and over a megaphone promised the passengers would be taken ashore and fed and then flown to the mainland. Not believing a word of this, a group of the refugees approached Captain Iaobacci and said they would kill him and blow up the ship if he didn't take them back to Vung Tau. Feeling as though he had no choice, he hoisted anchor and headed back to the resort headland down river from Saigon. Arriving there the next day, everyone was unloaded, including three babies who had been born onboard – now U.S. citizens since they had been born on an American-flagged ship in international waters.

Back at Phu Quoc, however, the situation was extremely grim. Vietnamese military authorities on the island refused to let refugees from any ship ashore. *USS Dubuque* was operating nearby and executed a humanitarian mission on April 6, sending boats with food and medicine, and later a doctor, to the *Pioneer Contender*. There, they found horrific conditions. Starving, desperately thirsty people on the merchant ship were also afflicted with extremely serious epidemics of multiple diseases causing nausea, vomiting, and the always-dreaded diarrhea, which further exacerbated their horrible dehydration and the sanitation situation. A small detachment of U.S. Marines led by Second Lieutenant Robert E. Lee and accompanied by a Navy hospital corpsman boarded the ship and did their best to maintain a semblance of order, but with many of the refugees being armed, the situation was extremely dangerous. On the third day at anchor, Lee's men were relieved by a new platoon under the command of Second Lieutenant J. Flores. Lee's horrific report to his superiors on the *Dubuque* motivated the American leadership to pressure the South Vietnamese to allow the refugees ashore, and on April 8, permission was received. It took three days to get them all ashore, and Lieutenant Flores counted the number of people disembarking from the 560 foot long ship at 16,700 people. Eventually about 40,000 refugees were put ashore at Phu Quoc. About a quarter of them were soldiers, who were quickly returned to the mainland to be assigned new units in the final defense of Saigon. The rest of the poor souls were left in squalid conditions on the island, but at least they were finally off the American ships. Presumably, most of them eventually found ways to get off the island, but little is known about their fate. Meanwhile, the *Dubuque* was released to return to duty with Task Force 76, joining *Benjamin Stoddert* and the other ships in port at Subic, awaiting what would be our orders to get underway again on April 18 for Vung Tau.

On April 30, the day the last Marines left the embassy rooftop, we had arrived at Phu Quoc to rendezvous with our friends on the *Dubuque* for what appeared to me and my shipmates to be an extremely sensitive mission.

As mentioned earlier, Operation Eagle Pull, the evacuation of Phnom Penh, Cambodia, had just been accomplished a few weeks earlier. Theoretically, then, all Americans who needed to be evacuated from that country were out and, theoretically, any Americans still inside the country were there because they chose to stay or because they still had work to do.

During the darkness hours of the morning of May 2, we found ourselves somewhere near the coastal border of Vietnam and Cambodia. I don't know if we were actually within the territorial sea of one country or the other, but that was moot because by this time *both* countries had fallen to the Communists and were therefore now "unfriendly" to Americans being there. Nevertheless, the *Dubuque,* with protective cover from *Stoddert's* guns, conducted a covert rendezvous with an inflatable boat carrying a small number of people – reportedly about a half dozen, and reportedly young Asian-Americans – who were taken aboard the amphibious ship. With the successful accomplishment of what one may very well assume was the extraction of intelligence operatives from Cambodia, both ships withdrew and *Stoddert* was released to return to Subic Bay. And it was none too soon, since our fuel supplies were dwindling and there was no hope of refueling at sea with all of the Task Force 76 ships having left Vung Tau.

With a long-established date for us to enter the Pearl Harbor Naval Shipyard for our much-needed overhaul, and with our hearts set on being home with our families soon, my shipmates and I felt we could breathe a sigh of relief since the war and the evacuation were over. All we had to do was make a quick stop in Subic and point the bow toward Hawaii.

If only it had been that simple.

CHAPTER 19

Midnight Mayday

COMMUNISTS TAKE OVER SAIGON; U.S. RESCUE FLEET IS PICKING UP VIETNAMESE WHO FLED IN BOATS

'HO CHI MIN CITY'
Communications Cut Soon After Raising of Victory Flag
By George Esper, The Associated Press

SAIGON, South Vietnam, April 30 – Communist troops of North Vietnam and the Provisional Revolutionary Government of South Vietnam poured into Saigon today as a century of Western Influences came to an end.

Scores of North Vietnamese tanks, armored vehicles and camouflaged Chinese built trucks rolled to the presidential palace.

The President of the former non-Communist Government of South Vietnam, Gen. Duong Van Minh, who had gone on radio and television to announce his administration's surrender, was taken to a microphone later by North Vietnamese soldiers for another announcement. He appealed to all Saigon troops to lay down their arms and was taken by the North Vietnamese to an undisclosed destination...

The transfer of power was symbolized by the raising of the flag of the National Liberation Front over the presidential palace at 12:15 today, about two hours after General Minh's surrender broadcast...

Broadcasting in the early hours of the Communist take-over, the Provisional Revolutionary Government's representatives said: "We representatives of the liberation forces of Saigon formally proclaim that Saigon has been totally liberated. We accepted the unconditional surrender of Gen. Duong Van Minh, President of the former Government."

The New York Times, New York, New York, Thursday, May 1, 1975

On the afternoon of Friday, May 2, we found ourselves released from duty with the *USS Dubuque* and steaming back down the eastern side of the Gulf of Siam (also known as the Gulf of Thailand), on our way to again round Hon Khai Island and make a pass along the coast off the Delta and Vung Tau to support any remaining refugee operations. The American fleet was already being dispersed to various ports or other duties.

What happened that day is best remembered in the following letter I wrote on the following day to my wife:

May 3

Dear Sharon,

The ship has been at sea now for over two weeks. Foremost on my mind is you. No mail at all has been received on board and little has gone out. I think of you. I dream of you and I yearn for you. Because of the lack of communications with you I haven't been very happy. I know your disappointed look as you open the mailbox and find it empty, and hate the thought of it. You don't know where I am or what I'm doing. I've wanted so badly to share my thoughts with you because of the past week has provoked much thought.

The whole Trauma of Vietnam is coming to a close for the United States but the human tragedy is all too apparent here now. Let me tell you the story of the end as I saw it. I'll start with right now, or rather with last night, then work back to previous events. At 1 AM this morning we rendezvoused with a S. Vietnamese patrol gunboat a hundred miles off the coast of Vietnam. The ship had a crack in the hull and was taking on water, sinking a foot an hour in spite of constant pumping. Her distress calls were reported to Rear Admiral Whitmire, the officer in charge of all evacuation efforts. The Stoddert was returning yesterday morning from Phu Quoc Island when we were directed by the Admiral to make best speed to help the Vietnamese ship, then 200 miles in the opposite direction, before she sank.

At 3:30 AM I went up to the Bridge for the 4-8 watch and was afforded an opportunity to witness a sad sight and story. The story first: Just before the defeat of SVN, the ship was ordered to sea. When the takeover of Saigon became imminent, the captain of the ship wanted to go back up the river to Saigon to pick up his wife and children and those of his crew. But some of the crew mutinied, led by a LTJG, and forced the captain at gunpoint to take the ship south to Phu Quoc Island, a trip of about 300 miles where they hoped they could safely leave the ship. When they arrived there, the mutineers left the ship to fishing boats instead of onto the island. By this time Saigon had fallen and a return there would be hopeless. They elected to try to reach Malaysia, the nearest safe haven. Then their world really fell apart. A hundred miles at sea, their 30 year old 150 foot ship developed a crack in the hull. They radioed their position, course, and speed and we were sent immediately since we were the only destroyer still at sea in the area of Vietnam. At 1 AM like I said we took their ship alongside and our engineers took a look to determine whether repair was feasible or towing the ship to Subic (1,100 miles) was worthwhile. Their engines and electronics were in excellent condition, but the hull was shot and the decision was made to scuttle her right there after salvaging whatever valuable gear could be removed, mostly electronics and 40 mm guns.

It was about this time that I came up on watch. After three hours of salvaging, a sad decommissioning ceremony was held by the Vietnamese crew. They stood in a somber formation and saluted as their flag (the flag of a country that in fact no longer existed) was lowered. Large holes were punched above the waterline port side aft and starboard side forward. The ship was deserted and the last man aboard opened the sea cocks (pulled the plug) in the engine room. She was cast off and then came the hour of slow circling, waiting for it to sink. The ship slowly sank, started to list to port and when the hole in that side hit the water she listed badly, the stern went down and the bow, in one last act of defiance rose straight out of the water before sliding quickly to the bottom, the air hissing out of the hole in the bow.

Aboard us now are 6 officers, 4 chiefs, 5 enlisted, a woman (the wife of the second in command) and her four little children. The captain of the ship was a personification of all that is sad in the end of the war. In three short days he had lost his family, his country, and his ship.

We're now on our way back to Subic but our job isn't done yet. The coast of Vietnam is now practically clear of U.S. ships where last week it teemed with them. Our last duty is to make a last swing around Con Son Island, the small Loran station off of the Mekong River Delta. There, no doubt, we will meet more refugee boats and will pick up all of those people desiring to go with us. This picking up refugees is not a pleasant task because they bring with them the sadness which is penetrating.

A word about the refugees. Merchant ships through the past few weeks have been used to transport these people to safe places. Due to the fact that these ships would pick up thousands of people at a time, the capabilities of the ships to provide for the people were totally inadequate. Hence the refugees were forced to live up on deck and the sanitary conditions were very poor and the food very limited.

Due to all the message traffic we received describing these conditions, when we took the crew of the SVN ship on board, the XO's planned accommodations weren't too pleasant. The woman and the children, the captain and the woman's husband were put up in the staff stateroom and the Commodore's Cabin which is good. But the XO has relegated the rest of the crew to the helo deck area, ordered them not to venture elsewhere and provided them with slop buckets. But sanity prevailed. This morning it became evident that such treatment of military men who had recently lost so much is barbaric. Lanny Benham (a Lieutenant Junior Grade – our missile division officer) *and John Brandl* (already introduced earlier as an Ensign and our assistant supply officer) *have done a lot to help them.*

Going over the XO's head to the captain, permission was obtained to let them inside the ship to eat, use the head, tour the ship, watch movies, etc. etc. Their laundry is being done and generally everyone is going all out to make them feel at home. It sort of revives my faith in mankind.

At any rate, if today we do pick up more refugees, we'll desperately need those RVN crewmembers to help communicate and organize.

Well, that's where we are now. We should arrive back in Subic probably by Tuesday, May 6. Once there we'll offload our passengers, their gear, pick up our mail and the equipment we left there on our swift departure the day I called you.

Sharon, I have a feeling that Subic will be packed with ships and one less will be hoped for. So I feel, as most of us do, that after a two or three day stopover, we'll leave for home. FOR HOME!

There's no way to be certain that this will happen. Changes have come fast and often lately. But, though it now seems that May 20 (arrival home) *is impossible, I hope and pray that we'll steam in through the Hawaiian surf before the end of May. I'm aiming for the 30th or earlier and that's my best guess for now.*

I have a longer story to tell you than this one that takes us through the events of the entire past two weeks. I'll tell it sometime after I have time to reflect on the implications of it all. Having been part of the end of the story of the Vietnam War, I've been part of history in a small way. It isn't something to be proud of but it isn't something to quickly forget. I won't.

Sharon, I want right now to hold you. I need your tenderness, your love, your... Just you.

I love you,
Jon

The RVN Navy ship whose crew we had rescued was the *RVNS Dienh Hai (HQ610)*, a hundred foot long, 122 ton patrol gunboat which had been transferred to the Vietnamese from the U.S. Navy in 1964, where it had been designated the PGM-69. Her mission was completed as she slid to the bottom of the Gulf of Siam, but my words about how helpful the crew might be were prescient. Our day, the last day in Vietnam, was just getting started.

CHAPTER 20

Always the Right Thing to Do

By the Associated Press

Workmen at military bases in Florida and Arkansas completed preparations Thursday for the arrival of South Vietnamese refugees, but legislation to finance relief effort for up to 80,000 persons hit a snag in Congress with rejection of a $327 million aid bill.

President Ford said the money was "desperately needed" to take care of the refugees. It was rejected by the House because it still contained authority for the use of American troops in already-completed evacuation operations.

Ford said the rejection was "not worthy of a people which has lived by the philosophy symbolized in the Statue of Liberty...

State Department spokesman Robert Anderson said that as of Thursday, the number of South Vietnamese evacuated by the United States totaled nearly 80,000. Several thousand other refugees fled to Thailand in South Vietnamese planes.

The more than 40 U.S. Navy ships which took part in the evacuation are headed away from the waters of Indochina, according to Secretary of Defense James W. Schlesinger.

Anderson said, however, that "as long as there are Vietnamese who come out (to the high seas) in distress, we will pick them up." Anderson said about 32,000 refugees had been picked up on the high seas as of early Thursday.

North Vietnam has demanded that all U.S. ships leave waters of the Vietnamese coast.

El Dorado News-Times, El Dorado, Arkansas, Friday, May 2, 1975

After taking the gunboat's crew on board, we steamed through the early morning hours of May 3, taking us closer to shore in order to make that "last pass" as we had been directed to do. Pete Hekman told me in recent years that we were also ordered to carefully watch our sonar for a "bottom contact." He said we were looking for the location of the C-5A's cargo hatch, which had fallen to the sea with Sergeant Dionne. There were reports that it had remained afloat for some time, before sinking to the sea floor, and the Air Force wanted to find it so it could, at some time in the future, be studied to better understand what had happened to cause that horrible crash. Our SQS-23 sonar was, for its time, very effective in detecting submarines, but with the caveat that no enemy submarine would be foolish enough to come within sonar range of our active pinging… something *no* self-respecting 1970's submariner would ever knowingly do. The South China Sea off the coast of Vietnam is fairly shallow and flat and we stood a good chance of detecting the hatch, so the order to try to find it was another reason for our last sweep through the coastal waters. But in spite of the best efforts of Chief Sonar Technician Irv Royal and the ASW team, the consensus among my shipmates with whom I've discussed this is that we failed to find it.

No sooner had I finished writing that letter in the mid-afternoon, we noticed a slow-moving boat on the horizon and altered our course to check it out. From a distance, it appeared to be a fishing boat with lots of people on deck. As we approached, the guys on our bridge with binoculars started to guess at how many there were, initially setting their estimate on a couple of dozen.

The boat's crew had seen us coming toward them and clearly altered their own course to intersect with ours. Its skipper wanted to make contact with a U.S. Navy warship. As we drew near, we could see our estimates of the number of people visible on board the small boat were far too low. Making our approach, we could see the boat's decks and superstructure were packed.

As we drew alongside the boat, which by this time had stopped its engines, it became clear that we were looking at well over a hundred people and they were of all ages, from little children to elderly women and men. It turned out there were 158 in all, including the boat's crew, and they were looking at us and calling to us across the water as their saviors. And they truly did need saving. The boat was a rusty tub, probably an old fishing boat, badly overloaded, and barely able to make any kind of speed through the water. Over ship-to-ship radio, we were able to determine they were desperate to be picked up because their boat was without food or water and extremely low on fuel. Even their small crew wanted to get off the boat, and they were all willing to go anywhere we were going, so long as it wasn't back to Vietnam.

Captain Hekman got on the radio to our operational commander who had, just the night before, sent us out to sea to respond to the May Day distress call of the gunboat. With our own ship extremely low on fuel, a situation made worse by our high speed sprint to get to the gun boat's location, one of the reasons we had been sent to pass along the coast was to look for refugees, and there was a tacit understanding that we would be authorized to pick up anyone we found. But here we were, facing the prospects of picking up 158 people, in addition to the gunboat crew we had already rescued, with very limited facilities to take care of that number of people for a couple of days while we returned to Subic Bay. So the captain explained the situation by radio to his superior officer in the chain of command and asked for guidance, anticipating direction to rescue these people. But he was stunned by the actual orders that came back.

He was told that the situation in both Subic Bay and Guam had just become extremely critical due to the number of refugees who had already reached port or were about to arrive on MSC merchant ships and Navy combatants. The maximum number of Vietnamese authorized by President Marcos to be on Philippine soil had already been exceeded. And our ship wasn't suitable to carry such a large number of people all the way to Guam, even if we had the fuel to do so. And we didn't. We barely had enough fuel to make it to Subic.

And so Captain Hekman was ordered to NOT bring these refugees on board. We were authorized only to provide the boat with food and water. But our captain could see these people were on a badly over-crowded vessel with abysmal conditions for sanitation or shelter. To make matters worse, the boat had only about one foot of freeboard (the distance from the water surface to the top of the hull), and all it would have taken to sink the boat was a single storm with moderate waves washing over the transom. *His absolutely correct judgment was that these people were likely going to die if we left them there on the boat.*

He then did something that I call heroic. Without further discussion with higher authority, the captain ordered that all of the people in that boat, including its crew, be brought on board. When I told him a few years ago that I was planning to write this story, he told me he saw it needed to be done and stressed that he was only doing his duty. He also said he couldn't conceive of being referred to as a hero. Lieutenant Commander Pete Finch, the XO, was also a highly professional officer, and he saw it as our duty to follow the orders we were given. So he did what he felt *he* needed to do. He told Captain Hekman that it was his opinion that he (the captain) would very likely face a court martial for disregarding orders, or at the very least he would be "relieved for cause."

I have always tried to follow a laughably simplistic – but poignant – personal motto: "Doing the right thing is always the right thing to do." If that's the quote I'm remembered for years after I'm gone, good! There off the coast of South Vietnam on that Saturday afternoon, we did the right thing, and it was indeed exactly the right thing to do. And even though he had argued against our doing it, Pete Finch went to work making sure we would do our best to get these people safely to the Philippines. And we did.

The RVN crewmembers we had rescued the previous night were enormously helpful in everything that followed, partly because the officers had good English language skills and were, therefore, able to convey instructions from our crew to their crew. But their enlisted men were also very helpful in searching the refugees as they came aboard, separating them from any firearms they were carrying – and many of them were armed. We also learned that some of the refugees were carrying large sums of money with them in case they had to buy their safety. Presumably, many had bought their way onto that boat, such was their dire situation. Attempts on our part to take this money, provide a receipt, and keep it safe for them until they disembarked weren't successful, which was understandable. They were more than willing to trust the U.S. Navy in giving up their guns (as if they had a choice), but they weren't going to be separated from the money they knew could be vital to them in starting new lives.

We got them all safely aboard and abandoned the boat, allowing it to drift. I sometimes wonder what might have happened to it. Would it be found and returned to service as a fishing boat or drift ashore somewhere? My best guess is that sooner rather than later it sank, justifying Pete Hekman's decision to rescue its passengers.

We had given the RVN sailors access to the facilities of the ship, but this wasn't practical for 158 new passengers. Our berthing compartments and "heads" were designed to just barely provide for the needs of our crew, since any extra room on board was there to house electronics, ammunition, equipment, food, and other consumable stores. Our first order of business was providing meals, shelter, and sanitation for the refugees in the only available space, which was topside. The aft end of the ship had a relatively open area because this was our small helo deck. Navy ships all have tarps in storage which can be broken out and rigged as a canopy over such an area to provide shade or rain cover for on-board ceremonies, such as a change of command event. So our Bos'n Mates went to work to build the best shelter they could, as rapidly as possible. Some of our crew generously offered up the thin mattresses from their own "racks" to allow the passengers on deck to have somewhere to sit or sleep. So far, so good.

The real challenge was providing for their need for private toilet facilities. Clearly, using buckets for this purpose would be unsanitary and simply inhumane. And so, our chief engineer Don Colley and his Hull Technicians (HT's), headed by Chief HT Bob Kelley, one of the most talented welders I've ever known, quickly designed and then built from sheet metal two simple and effective toilets. Basically, they were small steel platforms welded to the edge of the ship with their seat openings above the water. Each was surrounded by a shower curtain, which provided sufficient privacy to afford our guests some dignity – when dignity for them was a very short commodity. Happily, this arrangement worked pretty darned well.

Water was never an issue. A Navy steam-driven ship makes its own fresh water by using steam from its boilers to boil and distill seawater. The primary need for fresh water is to replace the water that leaks from the ship's boilers and engines, even though it's supposedly a closed system. The need for replacement water was constant any time we had boilers lit, and the crew was provided with just enough fresh water for drinking, cooking, showering, and laundry. Normally, we carefully conserved our fresh water to assure enough for the propulsion plant, so our showers had to be very short. (A "Navy shower" is to: Wet down quickly and turn off the water… soap up and scrub… and then quickly rinse off, all using the minimum water possible. Any "normal" shower when the water was left running, such as when in-port or off the ship, is referred to by Navy people as a "Hollywood shower.") But creeping back to Subic on only one boiler to conserve our fuel meant there was less demand for fresh water by the propulsion plant and therefore more than enough to provide for the needs of our guests.

Food was also not a problem. Captain Hekman was an early adopter of the concept of stocking the ship's food lockers with freeze dried food. Before this innovation became widespread in the fleet, food was generally limited to what came aboard canned, frozen (although ships have limited freezer capacity), or fresh. On *Stoddert* under Pete Hekman's command, we had our fair share of these foods, but we also had very healthy supplies of freeze dried stuff. So when faced with the challenge of feeding another 158 new "crewmembers," a number as large as half of our crew, our food service team stepped up to the job. Chief Mess Management Specialist K. P. Fernandez was a congenial and very hardworking guy and Captain Hekman respected him greatly.

At the first dinner, the refugees were desperately hungry. The captain knew it would be a challenge to maintain order so everyone could be fed without a riot, so he issued rifles to the Vietnamese Navy sailors to stand guard and organize a queue system for serving the meal. The passengers weren't aware, of course, that the RVN sailors' guns had no bullets. As the first tray of food was brought out from the galley, everything seemed well under control. Suddenly, one of the refugees pushed his way to the front of the line demanding to be served. As our crew and the RVN guards moved to pull the man out of the line, Pete Hekman got a better idea. He directed that the man be served from that first tray of food, which was simply rice, then sent off with his plate. Then, the captain motioned Chief Fernandez to continue service. His cooks brought out several more trays of rice, but there were also trays piled high with vegetables and meat. That bully was fed first, but not well, and the guards and other passengers made sure he was at the back of every food line for the rest of the trip. We learned afterward that he was a wealthy man who was used to being served and not used to sharing and being respectful of others. But times were changing fast and, as the Bible says, "The first will be last and the last will be first."

The rest of our trip back to Subic was relatively uneventful, considering the circumstances. Nevertheless, our last pass along the coast, within the territorial limits of Vietnam, was the very last U.S. military presence of the Vietnam War, which we were leaving in our wake on that afternoon of May 3, 1975.

One final note seems appropriate – and personal for me. Another terrible war had officially ended just under thirty years earlier. On September 2, 1945 in Tokyo Bay, aboard the battleship *USS Missouri*, the Japanese government formally surrendered to General of the Army Douglas MacArthur and the Allies. Under General MacArthur's signature on the formal document, with him signing as Supreme Commander for the Allied Powers, the next signature was that of Fleet Admiral Chester Nimitz, Commander of the Pacific Fleet and Pacific Ocean Areas. The five star Admiral's signature was the official acceptance of the surrender on behalf of the United States of America. On May 3, 1975, the very same day the *USS Benjamin Stoddert* sailed out of Vietnamese territorial waters to mark the end of the Vietnam War, on literally the other side of the world from us in Norfolk, Virginia, America's second nuclear aircraft carrier and the first of a new class of ships, the *USS Nimitz (CVN-68)* was commissioned. This enormous and powerful new warship bore both the name of the famous Admiral and, as its ship's logo, the circle of five stars he wore on his uniform's collar that day in Tokyo Bay.

The personal connection I mentioned was this: exactly ten years later in 1985, I found myself serving aboard *Nimitz* as its meteorological/oceanographic officer. I'm proud to say I was the first to officially have that position's title featuring both atmospheric and ocean science, even though I was still unofficially known throughout the ship as "the weather guesser." I served aboard *Nimitz* for two years and, although in that time we never conducted any actual combat operations, we were still very aware we were the pointy end of America's projected global power in the closing days of the Cold War. We served with honor in the summer of '85 as the base from which U.S. Delta Force special operations commandos conducted operations to free several of the American hostages who had been held for a long time by terrorists in Beirut, Lebanon. But that's another story for another day.

We were on our way home.

CHAPTER 21

Steaming Toward Dawn

The Last Refugee Ship Sails Into Subic Bay

SUBIC BAY, Philippines (UPI) – The last U.S. warship to leave Vietnam waters docked at Subic Bay today with 177 marooned South Vietnamese refugees, thus ending 11 years of American naval presence in that war-devastated country.

The guided missile destroyer USS Benjamin Stoddert, part of a U.S. 7th Fleet flotilla that evacuated refugees from South Vietnam, arrived at this American base, 90 miles northwest of Manila.

There was no official word on the arrival of a flotilla of South Vietnamese vessels with an estimated 30,000 refugees or whether it would dock at Subic Bay at all, a Navy spokesman said.

Among the refugees aboard the destroyer were remnants of a Vietnamese navy gunboat crew who had survived a mutiny aboard their vessel before they were picked up by the Stoddert.

The destroyer had completed its mission and was sailing to Manila when it was ordered to "make one last sweep of the evacuation area" off Vietnam, said Cmdr. Peter Hekman, the vessel's commanding officer.

The Berkshire Eagle, Pittsfield, Massachusetts, Tuesday, May 6, 1975

Stoddert was able to just barely make fifteen knots through the water on our trip to Subic Bay, the maximum speed possible on the one boiler we had lit. Between Captain Hekman and chief engineer Don Colley, careful calculations had been done to make sure we could make it to port without refueling, but it was going to be close. We didn't want to go any slower than we had to in order to get our refugee passengers off the ship as soon as possible. Even though we'd done everything we could think of to make it as comfortable for them as possible, it was still the South China Sea at low latitude at the cusp of summer. In other words, it was very hot and humid and the topside living conditions back aft were still pretty grim. But we were going to make it.

The little fleet of former RVN ships under the shepherding of the *Kirk,* and still under the overall command of Dick Armitage, had limited their own speed to about six knots in order to nurse their own fuel and to allow for preparations for their arrival in port to be made. Just outside of the harbor, we actually passed them – they were flying American flags by that time – and it was quite a sight. A more welcome sight, though, was the familiar entrance to the bay and the immediate prospect of tying up to unload people and pick up food and fuel for our return home.

Normally, a destroyer entering port at Subic Bay was sent to moor at "the destroyer pier," and generally in a nest of several ships tied up side by side, as we had been when we were sent to Vung Tau on April 18. But our orders from the local commander in the port were to proceed to the "carrier pier" adjacent to Cubi Point Naval Air Station, across the harbor from where we had expected to go. This was taken as a sign by XO Pete Finch, communicated already several times too often, but now one more time to Captain Hekman, that this was probably done so the other destroyers in port wouldn't see us lose our commanding officer. But Pete Hekman was made of sterner stuff and no doubt thought, "We'll see." He had no regrets about his actions.

In fact, there were no carriers in port. What we saw instead as we drew close to the huge, empty pier was a line of buses, which had been arranged to move all of the refugees we were carrying to their temporary living arrangements. Those arrangements had been made by the Lieutenant Commander (LCDR) who had been waiting at Subic for our return so he could come aboard in relief of Pete Finch as executive officer, who was due for a scheduled reassignment to his next duty station. There on the pier, looking up at us with a smile on his face, was LCDR Conrad C. Lautenbacher, Jr., a tall thin man who looked (at least to me) like he couldn't possibly be over twenty-five years old.

Pete Hekman wasn't about to get relieved of his command there at Cubi Point. This large pier was simply much better suited to allow us to dock directly alongside the pier so a gangplank (brow) could be easily rigged and our passengers safely disembarked. Pete Hekman and Pete Finch stood by the brow and oversaw a courteous, and orderly process of seeing our refugees across to the pier and aboard the buses. Where they eventually went, or where they are today, I guess I'll never know. But thanks to the courage and compassion of Pete Hekman and the hard work of our crew, they were no doubt off to find a far better world than the one they had left behind in Vietnam.

Our new XO, Conrad Lautenbacher, or Connie, as I now call him as a lifelong friend, was a superb officer. Parker T. Finch was a consummate professional and I salute him for his integrity and commitment to his duty, but I was to find in our new XO a guy who would match Pete Hekman's intelligent and professional management style. Oh sure, it was always an XO's job to be the bad guy, particularly if the CO wanted to play the good guy. But on our trip home and through the year ahead, I was very happy – and the crew was very lucky – to have *two* good guys. Connie, by the way, was on his way upward in his career. A Naval Academy grad like the captain and me, he had already served as a junior officer on a couple of ships, one of them an *Adams*-class DDG like *Stoddert*, and he had also just earned a PhD in Applied Mathematics from Harvard. Not surprisingly, he went on to command his own ship, the *USS Hewitt (DD-966)*, earn flag rank, and rise to a three star Vice Admiral. In that distinguished career, he served as Commander of U.S. Naval Forces in Central Command, based at Riyadh, Saudi Arabia for Operation Desert Shield and Desert Storm, and in his final tour in the Pentagon, he was Deputy Chief of Naval Operations for Resources, Warfare Requirements, and Assessments where he was in overall charge of Navy programs and the Navy's budget. Needless to say, we division officers on the *Benjamin Stoddert* got plenty of expert guidance and oversight from this very affable, intelligent, and detail-oriented XO. It wasn't always fun working for him, but he was a good teacher. And after retiring from the Navy, he continued to serve his country as the Under Secretary of Commerce for Oceans and Atmosphere, which means he was the Administrator of the National Oceanographic & Atmospheric Administration (NOAA), and he was my friend and customer when I was the corporate liaison to NOAA for my employer in my recent career in the aerospace industry. Since we were building weather satellites for NOAA and competing for new large contracts from the agency, my having worked for Connie Lautenbacher was just fine for both of us, although our friendship never led to any improper *quid-pro-quos.*

Back to our story, though. After remaining overnight at Cubi Point, we were directed to get underway the next day to move back over to the destroyer pier, and we had the privilege of tying up alongside *USS Kirk* and getting a close-up look at her menagerie of still-on-board helicopters on her bow, stern, and helo deck. She was quite a sight and, as we've seen, she had quite a story to tell, which was definitely a little more exciting than ours. But we still had much to be proud of and we were very fortunate. And, as far as we knew, nobody was talking about firing Pete Hekman for disobeying an order… we hoped.

From Wednesday, May 7 through Friday the 9th, we remained in

Subic, taking on stores. I think we shifted berths at least once more to let *Kirk* get underway to another pier where the helicopters could be taken off with cranes. But our time was spent loading supplies, making repairs, and drinking as many Subic Specials and San Miguel beers as possible in the last nights on liberty in Olongapo. For me, the quickly approaching deadline for completing the paperwork we needed for going into overhaul at the Pearl Harbor Naval Shipyard loomed large, and I redoubled my efforts while in port to complete the job. I was also in the final stages of relieving my friend Dave Rau as ASW officer, as he was due to leave the ship as soon as we arrived home. Since I was also going to relieve him as the nuclear weapons handling officer, there was a tremendous amount to learn – stuff that could get any number of people on the ship hurt, killed, or at least relieved if everything wasn't done *exactly* right.

And, of course, we were all thinking about our wives or girlfriend at home. Here's what I said to Sharon in my last letter before leaving for home:

Thursday, May 8

My Wife,

Tomorrow morning at 8 I start for home. I'm coming home finally after six and a half months of frustration, loneliness, and exhaustion. But through it all, Sharon, the driving factor in my days, the strength I needed was you. I know that you had a rough time in Hawaii living alone in our house, doing the finances, chores, and many of the things your husband should have done. But your courage to stay there is one of the many reasons that I'm so proud of you. I'd have been disappointed if you'd wanted to go back to Massachusetts because you were afraid and I'd also have been disappointed if you had breezed through the months with never a problem and never a complaint. In other words, I'm proud of your ability to take care of our home and I'm happy that I'm really needed for those areas a man is needed for. In two weeks it'll all be over. I want to never deploy again. But this deployment has proven what we already knew, that our love is perfectly strong and beautiful.

Another thing I want to say about these six months. Every "mail call" has proven me to be the luckiest man in the wardroom, right up to today. Today I received three letters and my care package. They had all had quite a voyage, crossing at least three or four different ships, finally being sent back to Subic from Singapore. But my goodies are still goodie and I love the hands that baked them. Sharon, I so love you it's incredible. Thank you for writing so often, for all the care packages, and for all the love.

(A couple of paragraphs about the anticipation of homecoming sex and other more mundane things are omitted here)

Sharon, this is my last sheet of paper. How fitting on our last night before heading home. I have the duty and must get dressed for watch now. Goodbye Olongapo!

Have a Happy Birthday, Sharon. (It would occur during our transit home.) *I wish so much I could be there but fear not, I'm practicing my singing (all five keys!) and you'll not miss that.*

We'll be in on the 21st if all goes well, that date being pretty firm now. I love to see you and hold you and love you.

Your husband,
Jon

P.S. Did you know UPI had a story about the STODDERT being the last warship to leave Vietnamese waters. Talk about being there when history is made!

CHAPTER 22

The Lady on the Pier

SAIGON (AP) – There are strange sights and sounds in Saigon today for someone who knew the South Vietnamese capital before the Communists took it over.

Soviet-built MIG jets that once engaged U.S. warplanes over North Vietnam fly in formation over Saigon in victory celebrations...

Ho Chi Minh's picture hangs from the presidential palace from which President Nguyen Van Thieu fled last month.

Maxim's the city's biggest night club, is now a police precinct station.

But some things haven't changed...

The Continental Shelf, the Continental Hotel terrace where prostitutes and pimps cater to foreigners, is back in full swing after being cleaned up briefly by the previous government. The Viet Cong and North Vietnamese seem to ignore the nightly show...

And Coca Cola is still an institution. It was served hot the other day at Tan Son Nhut when the North Vietnamese and Viet Cong bade farewell to the Hungarian and Polish delegations to the International Commission of Control and Supervision.

Jefferson City Post-Tribune, Jefferson City, Missouri,
Wednesday, May 21, 1975

Our transit to Hawaii was uneventful. We stopped at Guam for fuel and to offload much of our gun ammunition and missiles. Again, there seemed to be a chance that the captain's having disregarded an order about the refugees might still catch up to us and he'd be removed from the ship while there. And again, those fears were not realized. It was just a routine stop, although I wish I could have gotten off the ship to explore a little, there was no time.

We also stopped again at Midway Island. This time, I asked for and received special permission for a couple of hours off while we refueled to make a quick trip over to the airfield's operations building and the weather office. There, I again found my grad school classmate Charlie Mauck. He was happy to see me and we both jumped into his assigned Jeep (just like in the World War II movies) and drove the short distance to his living quarters so I could say hi to his wife, and also my friend, Linda. There was just enough time for them to open their freezer, which was packed with lobster tails. Charlie had taken up SCUBA diving, and they'd not yet gotten tired of eating as much lobster as they could ever want. Linda popped a couple of frozen tails in hot water, and in no time I was happily stuffing them into my mouth and washing them down with a cold beer. We then hopped back in the Jeep, and I got back to the ship in plenty of time before we shoved off. On the way, I got to see the hilariously awkward earth-bound antics of the great albatrosses, nicknamed "gooney birds" by the locals. Their mating ritual – clicking their bills together and then strutting around – was entertaining, as was their process of either landing or taking off – which was not very graceful. On the wing overhead, however, these beautiful birds are a spectacular sight to behold and a treat for any seaman who is lucky enough to see them. And I was very fortunate indeed to have had that brief "liberty call" on Midway and be the only person in the crew who had the opportunity to do something other than walk up and down the pier.

Homecoming day finally arrived: Wednesday, May 21. Arriving in mid-morning at the entrance to the channel leading to Pearl Harbor, we were met by a boat delivering the Pilot, who came aboard and was escorted to the bridge. Harbor Pilots all over the world are civilians who are very experienced mariners, normally former senior naval or merchant marine officers. They come aboard with their years of experience and local knowledge to assist ships in their navigation and tug boat use when entering or leaving ports. But that morning, the Pilot boat also delivered a happy surprise: a huge "flower lei" made of empty five gallon cardboard ice cream drums, colorfully painted, cut into "petals," and strung on a long piece of nylon line. Making a lei for the bow was the traditional way ships' wives clubs would prepare for Pearl Harbor-based ships' homecomings, and our ladies had worked hard on ours. We proudly placed our lei around our bow and then manned the rails in our spotless white uniforms for a slow, proud, transit up the channel. As we passed Ford Island in the middle of the harbor, just as on the day we left so many months earlier, we rendered the solemn and traditional honors to the *USS Arizona*, and then turned to the right, approaching the naval station pier.

For several days as we were nearing home, the captain was still considering the possibility of facing further scrutiny over having disobeyed an order. But he took it all in stride, believing he would know what to say, were he to face a court martial, about the dire situation and decision that he had made. He needn't have worried. An Admiral was on the pier all right: the Commander of Naval Surface Forces, MidPac Group. The silver embroidered stars shined from the gold shoulder boards on his own dress white uniform. *And he brought the band.* Our arrival at the pier was being treated like the homecoming of heroes. It turned out the United Press International (UPI) reporter who had written the piece I referred to in the P.S. in my letter to Sharon had interviewed the captain in Subic Bay. His piece, "The Last Ship Out of Vietnam," had been carried on the newswires and published in papers all across the country. Oddly, there was no article published in the Honolulu paper about our arrival, but one of the local TV stations had a news crew there to film the event.

But all that meant little to me. Even though I still didn't have a division to lead until I finished the final turnover with Dave Rau, which was now just a formality we would do the next day, I was pleased he had invited me to stand on the antisubmarine warfare (ASW) missile deck amidships with the ASW Division that I would very soon lead. So there I stood in my starched whites with "my men," and there on the pier was my lady! Sharon, my stunning and gloriously tan wife, had worn a crisp white dress with bare shoulders except for thin straps. She wore a lei of bright red carnations and was holding one just like it to place around my neck, just before the perfect homecoming kiss. She was the most beautiful thing I had ever seen (except for our wedding day) or have seen since (except for the births of our three children and two grandchildren). Her smiling face beamed up at me and everything was about to become very right in our world. Our lives together were about to begin all over again. And the war we had left in our wake was thankfully far behind us, but far from forgotten.

EPILOG: GOING DOWN FIGHTING

A Jacksonville, Fla., tugboat company's alleged negligence could ultimately take as much as $1.6 million out of the Brownsville economy.

International Shipbreaking Ltd., LLC has filed suit in U.S. District Court in Brownsville charging Smith Maritime was negligent in allowing the USS Stoddert to sink.

By Dwayne Harnett, The Brownsville Herald, Brownsville, Texas, May 9, 2001

Some ships just aren't meant to "become razor blades," the usual description of what happens to the scrap metal – *lots* of scrap metal – after retired ships are torn apart in shipbreaking yards. You've heard a lot about the *Benjamin Stoddert* and seen several references to our sister ship, the *USS Cochrane (DDG-21),* with its hull number just one short of ours. The *Cochrane* was named after Vice Admiral Edward L. Cochrane, a Naval Academy graduate who went on to receive a graduate degree at MIT and who advanced through the ranks as a naval architect to become Chief of the Bureau of Ships in 1942. His forward thinking about what the Navy would become after World War II had led to "modern" ship designs such as the *Adams*-class DDGs like his namesake and *Benjamin Stoddert.* But the two ships, which had shared a common design, called the same port home, and operated together so many times – including in Operation Frequent Wind – seemed like they were both heading toward an unavoidable destiny of shaving hair off faces and legs. Both were decommissioned in 1991 and sent to a mothball anchorage at the North Loch facility in an inlet opening from the west side of Pearl Harbor. There they remained, tied side-by-side and largely stripped of anything that could be useful for the newer ships coming into the fleet – in other words not very much – while awaiting the inevitable sentence of being towed somewhere to be scrapped. In early 2001, the time for the final voyage for these ships came at last. Sadly, *Cochrane* actually made it all the way to the scrap heap and the razor or new car factories. But *Stoddert* had a different destiny.

At the beginning of this book, I invoked the opening scene of the movie "Apocalypse Now," with its image of the Vietnamese coast being ravaged by explosions and fire, set against "This Is the End," hauntingly sung by Jim Morrison of The Doors. It may seem ironic, then, to tell you the last man to walk the decks of the *USS Benjamin Stoddert* was also named Jim Morrison. Clearly, we're not talking about the same person. One was a rock star who died tragically young, apparently done in by a lifestyle of hard drug and alcohol abuse. But the other is alive and well in Florida, a retired "old salt" whose amazing true story was told in his 2015 novella *Who Sank My Destroyer?* While I highly recommend reading his whole colorful account, currently available only in a digital version at Amazon.com, here are the essential elements of the story, re-told with the enthusiastic approval of THE Jim Morrison himself.

Although ready to sail, the oceangoing tug *Elsbeth II* sat in Pearl Harbor through the long Martin Luther King Memorial Day weekend in January, 2001. Because of the holiday, no Navy officials were available to sign off on the final transfer of the *Stoddert* and *Cochrane* to the responsibility of Smith Towing & Salvage Company of Green Cove Springs, Florida, the company hired to tow the two retired ships to Brownsville, Texas to be scrapped. But in mid-week, the 110 foot long yellow and black tug powered up her three 2,000 horsepower diesel engines and set off down the shipping channel to the sea. Behind her, *Stoddert* and *Cochrane* were under tow, the ships tied side-to-side. Smith Towing had filled a storage tank on each destroyer with 17,000 gallons of fuel, and placed on each ship a hundred feet of fuel hose. They had also secured a portable diesel fuel pump on the aft topside deck of *Stoddert*. The trip to the Panama Canal was expected to take about twenty five days and that extra fuel and gear was sure to be needed to augment the *Elsbeth II's* own fuel supply.

After clearing the channel and before heading on their southeasterly course, the crew cut the ships apart so they could be towed, unmanned, in single file, with *Stoddert* eight hundred yards astern of the tug and *Cochrane* another four hundred yards behind her sister ship. The steel towing cables between the ships were massive and heavy, but this was just business as usual for an open-ocean tow, one of the most challenging and dangerous jobs in the merchant marine service.

The tug's crew, captained by an old sea dog and Vietnam vet Navy SEAL named Glen Kern, included Jim Morrison as First Mate and Paul Torres, a qualified tug captain in his own right, who had flown out to Hawaii from Florida as a last minute addition to the crew. Also on board were an Engineer named Rudolf and a cook named Charley, both from Guyana. And, according to Jim Morrison, the final crew member was a parrot that cursed like a sailor and loved to sing opera! Jim had just celebrated his 62nd birthday on Christmas Eve during their time spent in Hawaii preparing the Navy ships for the tow, and he brought a lifetime of experience to the crew, experience that was to have a profound impact on what happened at sea.

I know from my own "ship-driving" experience that given an accurate and timely weather forecast, a fast warship can usually pour more steam into the turbines to kick up speed and choose the best course to evade a storm. But when you're in the middle of the Pacific on a slow moving tug trying to haul two destroyers, there's simply no evading the weather. You need to apply everything you know about ships and the sea and ride it out as best you can. And so, when a severe storm descended on the path of the *Elsbeth II* on her eighth day at sea, lashing her with more than thirty knots of wind speed, which kicked up waves over thirty feet high, life became hell for the crew. And to make matters worse, an accidental spill of most of the tug's fresh water into her bilges meant they had to either distill seawater into fresh using the ship's evaporator system or turn back to Hawaii. Unfortunately, the ship's fresh water maker was inoperative and hadn't been used in years – and they lacked a complete repair manual for the system. If the storm was a left hook to the jaw, their inability to make fresh water was a hard punch in the gut. The Engineer tried, but was simply unable to figure out how to get the distiller to work. Turning the three ships around and heading back to Pearl Harbor seemed like the only course of action available to them.

Since the tug and her tows were laboring along as best she could, unable to maneuver in the high seas, Jim volunteered to see what he could do to repair the unit, using skills he had learned as a Navy Machinist Mate early in his career. Day and night for several days, he kept at it, disassembling and reassembling the machine, but never getting anything but salt water from the output side. Then the break came when Jim came up with a new way of lining up the piping, and everything changed in an instant. Fresh water began to flow, and they knew they could continue slogging their way to Panama. But their biggest challenge was still ahead of them.

One morning at dawn, two weeks after the storm had hit them, still crawling along at very slow speed in high seas, they were shocked to discover *Stoddert* was sinking by the stern. Even though the crew had carefully inspected and tightly closed all the watertight doors and hatches on both Navy ships before they left Pearl Harbor, the *Stoddert* had suffered a leak. This could have come from a breach in the hull, which would have become thin after years of rust, making her vulnerable to the beating of the waves. Whatever the reason for this new crisis, it had to be dealt with quickly. If *Stoddert* went down with the tow cables connected, it could have severely endangered both the towing ship and the *Cochrane.* If they simply cut her loose, there was a good chance she would remain afloat, even if capsized, for an indefinite period of time, which would make her an unacceptable hazard to navigation for which their company would bear the responsibility.

The crew's options were limited, with none of them good. They used radio messages to discuss what to do with the ship's owner, Latham Smith, who had flown out to Hawaii to see them off but had since returned to the home office in Florida. Calls were made to the Navy to see if they would dispatch a fighter jet to sink her but the Navy, having made Smith Towing & Salvage sign off on taking responsibility for the ships, told them it wasn't their problem. But it was a big problem that needed to be solved, and fast. Cutting Stoddert free would be easy, but hanging around to see if she would sink wasn't an option. If they didn't keep moving toward Panama, they wouldn't have sufficient fuel to make it to shore, even with the extra fuel tanks on each of the ships being towed. And, of course, there was also a danger they wouldn't be able to recover and use the fuel stored on *Stoddert,* given the precarious situation with that ship.

The crew huddled and came up with a plan that would require all the skills they possessed – and luck they hoped they would find. Jim and Paul, who interestingly were not very fond of each other after having had adversarial situations arise in their common past, volunteered to go aboard *Stoddert.* Working as a team, they would assess the situation, including the status of their fuel tank, hoses, and the diesel fuel pump, and try to go through the entire ship opening and tying open as many watertight hatches and doors as possible. The plan was to work their way from the still-dry bow to the aft end which was already taking on water and sinking, with waves washing over the upper topside decks which held the aft five inch gun and the missile launcher and its magazine, and the small helo deck. The trick was to get this job done and off the ship as fast as possible before the sea flooded in and took her to the bottom of the sea. Neither Jim nor Paul had any interest in going down with the ship.

Wearing life jackets and equipped with flashlights, hand-held radios, pliers, and spools of wire to tie doors open, the two men were transferred from the bow of the rapidly heaving tug to the relatively more stationary main deck of the destroyer. Getting aboard was a harrowing experience, but Captain Glen put Jim and Paul safely on board amidships. As the tug backed away to a safe distance, the two made their way aft, pulling themselves hand over hand along the braided wire lifelines, to assess the situation. What they found was a terrible mess. Their pump was gone, washed overboard, and the hoses were strewn about the deck and hanging over the side. There was not going to be any way to salvage the fuel oil. So they headed forward and, taking turns, started going below into the pitch dark to open all the watertight openings, staying in radio contact with each other and with the skipper on the tug.

I remember all those doors and hatches very well from the hundreds of times I went through them in the course of three years on the crew. When we junior officers served as in-port command duty officers, it was our responsibility to tour the entire ship from stem to stern once during the night, going down into every engineering space and every major storage room and control center. We're talking about two dozen or so hatches and doors, all of which Jim and Paul were trying to open and, using the wire they had brought, make sure they stayed open. And all this while the ship was heaving unevenly in the seas and swell.

That danger manifested itself before they were done. A huge wave swept Paul overboard and, very lucky for him, Jim was able to grab him by the lifejacket as he swept down the side and haul him back aboard. Motivated by that very bad scare, they worked even harder and finally got the job done. In one more harrowing maneuver, they were safely plucked off the deck back onto the bow of the tug boat that had again nudged to the side of the now dying warship. Jim is proud to say he was the last man to step off the deck of the *Benjamin Stoddert.* Having survived this amazing ordeal, he and Paul became good friends from that day on. There's nothing like almost dying to make past animosity seem a lot less important.

The towing cables to both ships had been disconnected before all this maneuvering had begun, protecting the towing ship and the *Cochrane* from being pulled under the surface by the sinking *Stoddert.* The *Elsbeth II* re-rigged a tow cable to the now lonely *Cochrane,* and slowly circled the *Stoddert* for the remainder of that day. The great ship didn't give up easily. She had rolled onto her starboard side, still slowly sinking by the stern. But, like old, proud, war veterans sometimes do, the *USS Benjamin Stoddert (DDG-22),* finally stood straight up with her bow saluting the sky and, in Jim's words, "slid silently and gracefully beneath the waves." It was February 3, 2001, and the location was 7 degrees 56.5 minutes north latitude, and 140 degrees 38.7 minutes west longitude.

A four panel series of photos showing this final slide to the bottom of the Pacific Ocean were taken by the crew with a cheap camera – but good enough to be printed in *Newsweek* in a short piece written after interviews with the crew. Jim proudly told me he took those pictures and he generously granted me permission to reprint them in this book.

Without the spare fuel that was lost with *Stoddert*, the towing ship had to divert to Costa Rica to refuel before continuing their voyage to the Canal and onward to Brownsville. As you saw in the press clipping at the opening of this epilog, International Shipbreaking Limited (ISL), the salvage company in Brownsville, was pretty unhappy about the loss of revenue that would have resulted from selling off scrap from not one, but two old warships. So they sued Smith Towing & Salvage, also known as Smith Maritime, claiming negligence in losing the *Stoddert.* Business is business, after all, even if the executives of ISL would never know what it's like to handle a sinking ship in thirty foot seas.

In the lawsuit that followed, the United States Court of Appeals, Fifth Circuit found for Smith, the defendant. Their decision reading, in part:

After reviewing ISL's original complaint, we agree with the district court that ISL did not sufficiently plead an international tort claim. In its original complaint, ISL states that "Plaintiff's claim is for 'negligence' and 'breach of warranty of workmanlike service.'" The only reference to international conduct was made in a separate paragraph of the complaint: "During the voyage, the USS STODDERT was lost and/or was intentionally scuttled in the Pacific Ocean 'due to the negligence' and 'breach of warranty of workmanlike service' provided by Smith, its tug, and its crew. Although the pleading requirements under Rule 8 of the Federal Rules of Civil Procedures do not require an inordinate amount of detail or precision, we believe this single reference to international conduct couched in negligence and breach of warranty claims was insufficient to put Smith on notice of an international tort claim...

For the foregoing reasons, the district court's partial grant of summary judgment in favor of Smith is AFFIRMED.

The bottom line is that nobody ended up paying for what was an act of nature and unpredictably dangerous operations pitted against the unforgiving power of the sea. *USS Benjamin Stoddert,* having arrived at the sea bottom, hopefully intact because of her toughness, lies at peace out there on the Pacific's deep abyssal plain. As it should be.

My two great commanding officers Ed Siegrist and Pete Hekman will never be forgotten by those who served under their leadership and were enriched by their wisdom and integrity. Ed retired as a captain and I'm happy to say I had a chance to enjoy his company one last time at a Ship's Reunion in California in 2007 before he left us. I had the privilege of attending, and couldn't help but be deeply moved by, his very dignified internment ceremony at Arlington National Cemetery in early 2010. Pete Hekman is alive and very active in his retirement in the San Diego area. Like our XO Connie Lautenbacher, Pete ended his own impressive Navy career as a three-star Vice Admiral. He served his final tour of duty as Chief of Naval Material in Washington and went on to an extremely distinguished career in the nuclear engineering industry. I'm going to bet there's never been a better engineer that ever commanded a ship, or that managed the design and acquisition of new ships for the fleet.

The *USS Benjamin Stoddert's* story, and that of her distinguished early American namesake, are both important and it has been an honor to tell them. All wars are, of course, horrendous. They do terrible things to human beings and societies. And, as was the case with the Vietnam War, their endings can be very dark affairs. It has been an honor to write this story about that war's bitter end and our joyful return to our homes and our lives. I'm also very proud to be able to call myself a lifelong crewmember of a very special ship.

Post umbra lux: After darkness, light.

A COLLECTION OF IMAGES

All photographs were taken by the author, or by his shipmates, or are in the public domain, or are used with permission.

USS Benjamin Stoddert (DDG-22), aka The Benny Sweat

The Honorable Benjamin Stoddert of Maryland, the USS Benjamin Stoddert's Crest, and the author

Commanding Officers Ed Siegrist and Pete Hekman

The First *USS Stoddert (DD-302)*

Wounded Warrior – Direct Hit
Sister Ships *Benjamin Stoddert (DDG-22)* and *Cochrane (DDG-21)*

CO Ed Siegrist and XO Pete Finch Enjoying a Show at Sea

Boat Crew Bos'n Mates Frankie Taranovich and Mike Lucci

Aboard the ROK Ship
Chung Buk
Captain, Commodore, and Ensign

Thanksgiving Evening in a Chinhae Coffee Shop
Future Ambassador Chung Dal-Ho and the Author

Change of Command: Old Salts and Young Salts
Commander Ed Siegrist Speaks While Commander Pete Hekman Awaits Assumption of Command, March 8, 1975
Stateroom-mates Jon Malay and John Brandl at the Ceremony.

Air Force C5A Galaxy Crewmember Staff
Sergeant Donald Thomas Dionne, Sr.

Executive Officer Pete Finch and the Crew of the South Vietnamese gunboat watch as its captain is the last to leave his ship and a solemn decommissioning at sea is held before she is scuttled

RVNS Dienh Hai (HQ610)

The 2nd in command and his family

Our Vietnamese guests

Captain Pete Hekman (top left center) saying goodbye to the refugees at Subic Bay

Pearl Harbor Homecoming Welcome

Eyes only for each other

A happy scene screen-grab from local TV coverage of the homecoming

Some of the officers of the *Stoddert* wardroom
after return from the WestPac deployment

(From L to R): LT Don Colley (Chief Engineer), LTJG Jim Moseman (Missile Officer), LTJG Jon Malay (ASW Officer); LCDR Conrad Lautenbacher (Executive Officer); CDR Pete Hekman (Commanding Officer); ENS Rick Knock (Gunnery Officer**); LT Rick Buttina (Weapons Officer); LT Eric Utegaard (Operation Officer); and LT Jim Coker (Supply Officer**)*

*Reported aboard just before the ship's return home to Pearl Harbor
**Reported aboard after this story

Sinking of the decommissioned *USS Benjamin Stoddert*

(Photos by Jim Morrison. Used with permission.)

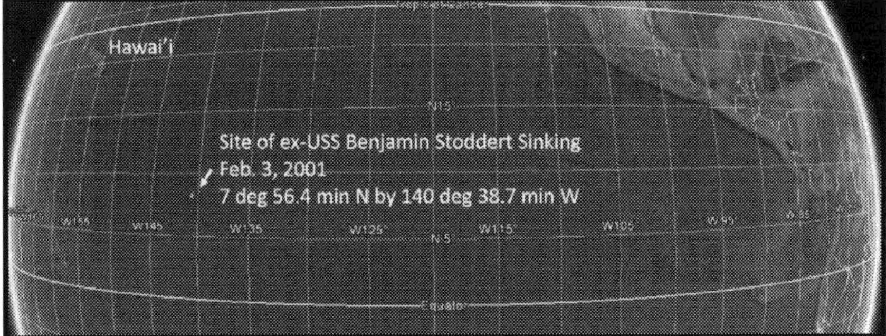

ACKNOWLEDGEMENTS

I want to thank my fellow officers of the *USS Benjamin Stoddert (DDG-22)* with whom I've spoken or corresponded, including: disbursing/assistant supply officer John Brandl, chief engineer Don Colley, communications officer Pete Coste, executive officer Conrad Lautenbacher, damage control assistant Jim Moseman, gunnery officer, Dave O'Neill, and operations officer Eric Utegaard. Our navigator, Jim Farrens, helped with the details of our timeline and his encouragement and friendship were of immeasurable help. It was truly an honor to serve with all of these gentlemen and I ask them to forgive me if I've forgotten or misstated some of the facts.

A very special thank you to my commanding officer during the last three critical months of the deployment, Vice Admiral Pete Hekman, USN (Ret.). He was a very tough boss to please, but also far and away the best one I ever had. I truly hope I got this story right for this man I admire so greatly.

I want to also acknowledge all of the great enlisted men and Chief Petty Officers of the *Benjamin Stoddert* with whom I served. I apologize I've not mentioned many of their names in these pages, but these men were hard working, good natured, and professional. The officers may "drive the ship," but the white hats and chiefs "run the ship."

Thanks to Jamie Hawkins, my friend and colleague at NOAA and now at Lockheed Martin, for his excitement about listening to my sea stories and his relentless exhortations to get these stories into a book. And thanks to another friend, Ed Goldstein, for his professional editing and encouragement.

I guess thanks are in order for the anonymous staffer at the National Archives who had the unenviable task of photocopying hundreds of pages of the *Stoddert's* deck logs – even though I had to wait over a year and then pay a goodly sum to get them.

Thank you to my smart and talented daughter Kate, the very best writer and editor I know, for her careful editing. Her polish makes the brass work of this book shine! And thanks also to my other talented and smart daughter, Liz, and to my son Ben, a fellow naval officer and space-guy. All three of them have listened to my sea stories all their lives. I hope they enjoy this loving re-telling of them this one last time.

Thank you to Stewart Hopewell, a great son-in-law and talented artist, for designing the cover.

But most of all, I want to thank my wife Sharon, my "Lady on the Pier." Much of this book is our story, and to help me tell it, she had saved the letters I'd written to her from the ship over forty years ago as the events unfolded. She graciously allowed me to quote from them, even though they were originally classified "For Your Eyes Only!" She encouraged me to not give up on this project and also gave me a tough but loving first edit of the book. It's the loving part I'll always appreciate the most!

And finally, I need to acknowledge my tremendous respect and appreciation for the late Captain Ed Siegrist, my first commanding officer. I hope he'd be proud of this book and of the Navy career of the young Ensign he helped to shape through his truly great leadership and example. I think of him every time I look up to the clouds, either as a meteorologist or as a daydreamer, and see "the back of the front."

SOURCES AND RECOMMENDED READING

Boyne, Walter J. *Beyond the Horizons: The Lockheed Story.* New York, NY: St. Martin's Press, 1998.

Chairman, United States Joint Chiefs of Staff. *NEMVAC (Non-combatant Emergency & Evacuation Plan) SURVEY REPORT 4-19 MAY 1975.* Washington, DC: Excised Version, 1980

Healey, Frank H. *The Battle of Chelsea Creek.* Published in *The Historical Collections of the Danvers Historical Society,* Volume XLVII. Danvers, MA: 2005

Herman, Jan. *The Lucky Few: The Fall of Saigon and the Rescue Mission of the USS Kirk.* Annapolis, MD: Naval Institute Press, 2013

Isaacs, Arnold R. *Without Honor: Defeat in Vietnam and Cambodia.* Johns Hopkins University Press, 1983 (New Edition 1998).

Karnow, Stanley. *Vietnam, a History: The First Complete Account of Vietnam at War.* New York, NY: The Viking Press, 1983.

Morrison, Jim. *Who Sank My Destroyer? USS Benjamin Stoddert (DDG-22)*: Kindle Edition. Amazon, 2015.

Palmer, Michael A. *Stoddert's War: Naval Operations During the Quasi-War with France, 1798-1801.* Annapolis, MD: Naval Institute Press, 2000.

Thomas, Evan. *Sea of Thunder: Four Commanders and the Last Great Naval Campaign 1941-1945.* New York, NY: Simon and Schuster, 2006.

Toll, Ian W. *Six Frigates: The Epic History of the Founding of the U.S. Navy.* New York, NY: W.W. Norton & Company, 2006

Veith, George J. *Black April: The Fall of South Vietnam 1973-1975.* New York, NY. Encounter Books. 2012

Printed in the United States
By Bookmasters